Alexander (Sandy) Noble was born in London in 1954 and was educated at Charterhouse and Oxford. He began his career in Washington D.C. before returning to the UK in 1980. He worked for several well-known publishers including Pergamon Press and Penguin Books before gaining an MBA at the London Business School in 1988. Since then he has been entirely freelance, working on several Euro-projects and contributing to the *European* newspaper. Apart from writing he is also involved with the IndEUR series of European stock market indices and is a director of an avant garde jazz CD company.

FROM ROME TO MAASTRICHT

The Essential Guide to the European Union

Alexander Noble

WARNER BOOKS

A *Warner* Book

First published in Great Britain by Warner Books 1996

Copyright © Alexander Noble 1995

The moral right of the author has been asserted.

A CIP catalogue record for this book
is available from the British Library.

ISBN 0 7515 1574 4

Typeset by Solidus (Bristol) Limited
Printed and bound in Great Britain by
Clays Ltd, St Ives plc

Warner Books
A Division of
Little, Brown and Company (UK)
Brettenham House
Lancaster Place
London WC2E 7EN

Contents

CONTENTS

CONTENTS

Author's note

The 'European Community' has changed dramatically over the years. It started with the European Coal and Steel Community (ECSC) in 1951, which was joined by the European Economic Community (EEC) and the European Atomic Energy Community (Euratom) in 1957; the Treaty of Paris and the Treaties of Rome were the respective founding documents. These 'Communities' all existed alongside each other before becoming the European Communities (EC) – confusingly generally referred to as *the* European Community – established by the 'Treaty Establishing a Single Council and a Single Commission of the European Communities' (the 'Merger Treaty') of April 1965. The Single European Act followed in 1986, laying the groundwork for the '1992' initiative. This was followed by the 'Treaty on European Union' (commonly referred to as the 'Treaty of Maastricht') in February 1992. Because these different titles can lead to confusion I refer to the 'EU' (the European Union) rather than the other acronyms, except where provisions referred specifically to either the EEC or the EC or where it is clearly anachronistic to do so. The Maastricht Treaty changed the official name of the European Communities to the 'European Community', and this, subsuming the old Communities, still exists, but as one of the 'three pillars' of the EU. The Treaty of Rome is still extant and has been supplemented and revised by the Single European Act and the Maastricht Treaty, and a series of less well-known treaties in between. Its original provisions, except where superseded or added to, still stand and effectively act as the constitution of the EU.

Peace through Trade – a Prophecy

'By the proposed Free Trade Union some part of the loss of organisation and economic efficiency may be retrieved [which had been caused by the splitting of Europe into numerous independent states, with all the complications that portended for trade organisation, as each country set up its own tariff regime], which must otherwise result from the innumerable new political frontiers now created between greedy, jealous, immature, and economically incomplete, nationalist States. Economic frontiers were tolerable so long as an immense territory was included in a few great empires; but they will not be tolerable when the empires of Germany, Austria-Hungary, Russia, and Turkey have been partitioned between some twenty independent authorities. A Free Trade Union, comprising the whole of central, eastern, and south-eastern Europe, Siberia, Turkey, and (I should hope) the United Kingdom, Egypt, and India, might do as much for the peace and prosperity of the world as the League of Nations itself. Belgium, Holland, Scandinavia, and Switzerland might be expected to adhere to it shortly. And it would be greatly to be desired by their friends that France and Italy also should see their way to adhesion.

'It would be objected, I suppose, by some critics that such an arrangement might go some way in effect towards realising the former German dream of Mittel-Europa. If other countries were so foolish as to remain outside the Union and to leave to Germany all its advantages, there might be some truth in this. But an economic system, to which everyone had the opportunity of belonging and which gave special privilege to none, is surely absolutely free from the objections of privileged and avowedly imperialistic schemes of exclusion and discrimination. Our attitude to these criticisms must be determined by our whole moral and emotional reaction to the future of international relations and the peace of the world ...

'... must we not base our actions on better expectations, and believe that the prosperity and happiness of one country promotes that of others, that the solidarity of man is not a fiction, and that nations can still afford to treat other nations as fellow creatures?'*

These words were written not in the 1990s, by someone who even now would be considered as highly visionary, but in 1919, immediately after what was then regarded as the worst war in human history. The issues and fears it addresses are with us still, especially since the break-up of the former Soviet Union and the reunification of Germany, and for all the changes in prose style it could be addressing recent developments such as the division of Czechoslovakia and the civil war in former Yugoslavia. Keynes clearly supported the proposition that free trade is a force for peace. It works in tandem with political institutions – in his case the League of Nations, in ours the Community – to promote a more prosperous, and thereby a safer and more peaceful world.

* John Maynard Keynes, 'Proposals for the Reconstruction of Europe', Chapter VII, Remedies, 1919, under *Essays in Persuasion*, First edition 1931, Royal Economic Society, Macmillan Press, London 1984.

Introduction – a Brief Historical Sweep

Europe now permeates our lives. In Britain feelings towards it cross the party political divide and there are Europhiles, Europhobes and Eurosceptics in all the major parties. Fishermen, in Spain as well as Cornwall, and butchers in Athens as well as Aachen have to abide by its quotas and standards; banks, insurance companies and telephone companies can now in theory sell the same services in Denmark and Spain as in the United Kingdom; trucks can take tomatoes from Taranto to Stockholm with minimal border formalities. As a UK resident, in theory you can buy a share in a French or German company using a bank account in the Netherlands with no more formalities than you experience in the United Kingdom (though you are still unlikely to do so because differing national legislation, bank charges, stock-exchange rules, etc. would probably make it too time-consuming and probably expensive). The water you drink is supposed to meet minimum standards set by the European Commission; health, safety and worker protection (apart from in the United Kingdom) are all supposed to reach common, higher standards.

The idea of 'Europe' is so pervasive that politicians in all countries treat it either as a vision or nightmare depending on which policies they wish to promote to their local electorates, and individuals, companies and pressure groups can apply to the Commission or the Court of Justice when they feel that their national institutions have not dealt correctly with them. But how did it all start? A common perception of Europe goes back millennia. After all, the very word is the name of a Phoenician princess in Greek myth, and it is tempting to think the first two letters 'e' and 'u' form the ancient Greek word for 'well' – 'eu'! The Romans then provided a degree of consistent civilisation and order over virtually the whole continent, bar Germany and the far north. Their civic control decayed with their military power, but gradually the Roman Catholic church assumed the Emperors' mantle, in that its mission knew no borders and its furthest outpost answered to Rome, in theory at least. It also provided a parallel and alternative authority and hierarchy to the existing secular order. Like the EU, it too impinged on the activities of European kingdoms, and many were the disputes between the secular authorities and the spiritual.

The idea of a unified Europe was revived by Charlemagne, fully conscious of the past, adopting the title of Holy Roman Emperor on Christmas Day 800. A series of German emperors tried to keep the flame alive, though for most of the time their 'empire' consisted of some pomp and fitful control over what is now Germany, punctuated by sporadic attempts to control parts of Italy. The Spanish, under Charles V and Philip II, tried to restore the imperial position but the task was beyond them. Napoleon was the next person to make what might be described as a serious attempt to unify Europe, even though he abolished the title of Holy Roman Emperor. His violently executed dream began to fall apart in the flames of Moscow, and ironically the only change to the political map after his fall was less unity, not more, with the appearance of Belgium as a new nation state in 1830.

The nineteenth century was the era in which what we recognise as the modern nation state came into being, the process being completed in Western Europe with the internal unification of two peoples, the Italians and the Germans. For the first time in history, Western Europeans (still with a few exceptions) owed their loyalty and their self-definition politically to what they regarded as a nation. Thus 'Italian' or 'German' ceased to be geographical and became political expressions. 'European' remained a geographical expression.

In a sense, the process of centralisation and homogenisation of political structures occurred, but only within discrete limits, i.e. general linguistic or territorial borders. And the nation states that developed started with very different political systems, some of which allowed for decisions to be made by very small groups of people who did not necessarily have the intellectual powers or personal characteristics to make wise political decisions. Even the democratic nations tended to operate an even more limited form of democracy than that under which we live now. All tended to share an extreme centralisation of power which, with limited communication and little understanding of each other, and with different aims and ambitions which were never truly aired, was a recipe for all sorts of friction becoming conflict.

Thus in August 1870, on a sunny summer's day, the Prussian army, with its German allies, marched into France. The reasons for going to war – over who would succeed to the Spanish throne – would now seem ludicrous to Europeans, but the world was then a very different place, with democracies in Europe a minority. Bismarck, the German Chancellor, provoked the French Emperor, Napoleon III, into declaring war, even though France was manifestly unready for it. So started the Franco-Prussian war.

Germany was the new colossus on the European stage; the geographical nation had come together through the *Zollverein* – a customs union which removed internal trade barriers – and the offensive and defensive alliances signed during the Franco-Prussian war by the four southern German states remaining outside the Northern German Confederation. Formal unification was achieved in 1871, with the crowning of the Kaiser at Versailles and the political inclusion of the southern states. Economically, Germany, as a united nation, was the most powerful state in Europe, overtaking the United Kingdom in many industrial fields. Like any newcomer, it wanted to make its presence felt, and was prepared to use its daunting economic power to build the strongest military forces in Europe. It was theoretically ruled by the autocrat Kaiser Wilhelm I, though real power was in the hands of Bismarck who ran the country in an absolutist manner. There was an elected parliament, the Reichstag, but this did little to curb his activity. The regime was philosophically underpinned by the writings of Hegel, with duty to the state being a citizen's highest obligation in return for which the state undertook to see to the citizen's material needs. (The bargain was kept on the state's part by the provision of welfare services.) Bismarck was one of the wiliest politicians in Europe, with a firm grasp of what would now be called *Realpolitik*, setting up alliances that counterbalanced any threats to the new nation. His essential aim was to preserve and expand Germany's power, using any means including the military; Prussia, the dominant state in the new Germany, had already fought a war with Austria, the previously dominant power in Germany, over Schleswig-Holstein. By the end of 1871, the other German states and principalities had joined Prussia to create what we would now regard as the nation of Germany.

The creation of this new state (and to a lesser extent the unification of Italy) caused a fundamental shift in the balance of power in Europe, and a major realignment among European nations, with France and Britain becoming allies and the smaller states such as Belgium and Holland becoming determined neutrals.

So began what some historians have regarded as seventy-five years of European civil war. Revenge for the humiliation of 1870–71 was a major concern for France in the First World War, and the issue of reparations had the same effect for Germany in the lead-up to the Second. The defeat of Germany in the Second World War was achieved by Russia and the United States of America, thereby ending Europe's militarily predominant position which had endured for four centuries. The victors in 1945 were not interested in the revanchism that had characterised the interwar periods of 1871 to 1914 and 1918 to 1939. Russia wanted a buffer between itself and any future German aggression (Germany had invaded it in both World Wars) and achieved this by installing sympathetic and clearly subordinate regimes in the countries of Eastern Europe – Poland, Hungary, Bulgaria, Romania and Czechoslovakia – and by holding on to the eastern half of Germany itself in the form of the German Democratic Republic. The United States wanted a reasonably strong Europe to act as a deterrent to potential Russian expansionism, and this encouraged it to institute the Marshall Plan to accelerate European and, in particular, German recovery. The North Atlantic Treaty Organisation (NATO) was set up to provide an effective conventional deterrent. Eastern European states did not benefit, because even though not all of them possessed Russian-imposed regimes, the message from Moscow was to avoid American influence.

The devastation of the war, and the recognition that Europe's pre-eminence had been lost, led to some sober thinking among European politicians, and more specifically by some men of vision: Jean Monnet, Robert Schuman, both French, and Konrad Adenauer, the German Chancellor. The economic failures of the interwar period in the 1920s and 1930s, rampant inflation in Germany, high unemployment and industrial and social unrest there (and in France, Britain and Italy) were seen as directly contributing to the rise of Nazism and the Second World War. To avoid a repetition of the nightmares of the past and, in the long term, to rebuild Europe's position in what was now a bi-polar world, they determined to link their countries with such strong economic ties that future hostilities would be inconceivable. In September 1946 in Zurich, Winston Churchill, no less, urged Franco-German reconciliation, even using the phrase 'United States of Europe'.

Jean Monnet, the General Commissioner for France's Modernisation Plan, prepared a briefing paper for Robert Schuman, the French Foreign Minister, which led to the Schuman Declaration, a draft of which was sent to Konrad Adenauer, who approved with enthusiasm. Schuman's vision was clear:

World peace cannot be safeguarded without the making of creative efforts proportionate to the dangers which threaten it.

The contribution which an organised and living Europe can bring to civilisation is indispensable to the maintenance of peaceful relations . . .

Europe will not be made all at once, or according to a single plan. It will be built through concrete achievements which first create a *de facto* solidarity . . .

The Declaration was presented on 9 May 1950 and augmented at an Intergovernmental Conference in Paris in June 1950, which led in turn to the Treaty of Paris founding the ECSC in April 1951. There are four basic principles behind the treaty:

(a) the superiority of institutions; institutions become repositories of experience, in a way that no individual can.
(b) the Community is independent of the Member States which founded it, both politically and financially.
(c) Community institutions are set up so that all – Council, Commission and European Parliament – are involved in the decision-making process.
(d) Member States are equal within the Community.

And so, the first step on the road to European economic integration was taken and the European Coal and Steel Community came into being. Its preamble is instructive:

Recognising that Europe can be built only through practical achievements which will first of all create real solidarity and through the establishment of common bases for economic development . . .

Resolved to substitute for age-old rivalries the merging of their essential interests; to create, by establishing in economic community, the basis for a broader and deeper community among peoples long divided by bloody conflicts; and to lay the foundations for institutions which will give direction to a destiny henceforward shared . . .

CHAPTER I

The European Coal and Steel Community (ECSC)

The driving ideals that lie behind the European Union were set out as long ago as 1951 in the Treaty of Paris, which laid down the terms for the European Coal and Steel Community.

Article 2 states that the ECSC 'shall have as its task to contribute in harmony with the general economy of the Member States and through the establishment of a common market ... to economic expansion, growth of employment and a rising standard of living in the Member States'. Thus, right from the start, key aims were set out: 'common market', 'economic expansion', 'growth of employment' and a 'rising standard of living'. There has been no deviation from these aims in the interim. They have been augmented by more recent concerns – the environment, social justice – and political as well as economic union, but they still drive the ethos of the Union.

The ECSC is concerned with the two specific industries of its title but its provisions, *mutatis mutandis*, can be applied to the broader common market. It is quite specific in Article 3, where the intention to establish a level playing field is clearly laid out; suppliers are not to create artificial shortages nor to deny any customer access to production. Competition is to be encouraged within an orderly market to ensure that prices are the lowest possible. Import and export duties and tariff and non-tariff barriers within the Community were abolished, as were restrictive practices such as cartels or discriminatory pricing. Non-tariff barriers consist of such things as quotas, import/export bureaucracy; a classic example of this was the French anti-Japanese video-recorder action, whereby France established a small customs post in Poitiers – not the most accessible of French towns, at least to goods arriving by sea – where a small staff of *douaniers* individually processed each VCR. It was not actually a quota, but it was definitely a bottleneck which slowed down imports to a trickle.

The European dimension is covered by clauses that encourage international trade and the modernisation of the two industries, so that the different countries are able to compete with equivalent plant. Nor does the Treaty forget the proper use of resources and the status of the workforce: the Community is to 'ensure the maintenance of conditions which will encourage undertakings to expand ... using natural resources rationally and avoiding their unconsidered exhaustion'. The Community's role is active, providing 'guidance and assistance', financial help with restructuring and monitoring the markets. An important principle was also established, namely that the Community assumed corporate powers, that is it became a legal entity just as when one incorporates a company, thereby conferring legal 'personality' on what is in reality an abstract entity; as we all know, a company has a separate legal existence from those who work in or for it. It needs to be incorporated so that it can draw up contracts, take on debt, sue and be suable, in other words have the same rights and liabilities as an individual.

The Commission is responsible for keeping an eye on market and price trends, for drawing up programmes for modernisation and for keeping itself abreast of technical developments. It is also responsible for ensuring that provision is made for workers made unemployed through modernisation, and can grant aid to stabilise their incomes during periods of structural change, or to resettle or retrain them. Furthermore, the Commission is capable of granting loans for investment programmes and can demand information from producers so as to be able to co-ordinate their activities. In other words, it was intended right from the beginning that the Commission should take an active, almost interventionist stance, from a perspective that saw the European coal and steel industries as a whole. The EU spent 3 billion ECU between 1954 and 1988 on the European coal industry to help unemployed miners towards early retirement or new jobs and during that period reduced the number employed in the industry by 180,000 (62 per cent of the workforce).

The steel industry especially was considered when the treaty was signed to be a flagship industry, rather as airlines, tele-communications and car industries are now: a nation could not be considered a nation without possession of such industries. Conse-quently, even though new materials and more efficient use of steel led to stagnant or falling demand, steel-producing nations still maintained old, inefficient plant, while often adding new, and subsidising both (the former obviously more so) in the consequent glut. There were, of course, important political and social con-siderations – the steel industry was a major employer. The Commission was therefore intended to be a supranational arbiter, which would supervise the industry, and impose quotas where necessary and draw up production programmes. National sub-sidies were banned outright, and the Commission had the power to impose substantial fines on those who broke this rule. It is not always easy to separate out subsidies from, for example, a government granting 'vocational' or retraining aid or building up stocks of unwanted product or paying excessive prices or subsidis-ing other inputs (e.g. for coal and steel, transport and energy costs) or applying a favourable tax regime. It was the Commis-sion's job to root out this sort of behaviour, and making it the supreme organiser of the industries' production was the most obvious way to do this. The level playing field is expressed in Article 60, where the following are prohibited:

> ... unfair competitive practices, especially purely temporary or purely local price reductions tending towards the acquisi-tion of a monopoly position within the common market; discriminatory practices involving, within the common market, the application by a seller of dissimilar conditions to comparable transactions, especially on grounds of the nationality of the buyer.

Other provisions set out for the ECSC were:

— Sale conditions had to be made public.
— Cartels agreeing prices were banned as were production
agreements (i.e. restrictions on supply to keep prices up).

Qualified workers could seek employment in any of the Member
States once common definitions of qualifications were established.
Different rates of pay for migrants and nationals were prohibited.
The Commission could try to match labour shortages in one
Member State with surpluses in another.

The success of the EU in restructuring the steel industry has
been limited. Quotas were progressively reduced, but always, it
seems, less quickly than demand fell, thus constantly leaving a
surplus. Other industries that might have helped maintain
demand, shipbuilding for example, are in decline in Europe as
Japanese and then Korean competitors drove them out of business.
And the car industry uses less steel as it substitutes plastics and
other materials in the search for lower weight (e.g. Audi now
produces an aluminium-bodied car) and greater fuel economy. An
ECU 1 billion programme is currently running (1992–95) to
reduce capacity by a further 25 million tonnes per annum and to
pay for the expected 50,000 redundancies. At the Essen summit
of December 1994 it was proposed that the following five-year
plan should include cuts of another 25 million tonnes, but cuts of
19.4 million were finally agreed.

Just as the ECSC prefigured so much that was in the Treaty of
Rome, so in other senses it has prefigured much of what has
happened in the EU. Member States are members voluntarily
(even if more and more inextricably) and it can be difficult to agree
the enforcement of hard-headed decisions such as the cutting of
production. So issues that should have been resolved many years
ago continue to fester but, as there is a sense that political
momentum must be maintained, the EU broadens its areas of
competence, hoping perhaps to tidy up the loose ends, like excess
coal and steel capacity, retrospectively.

CHAPTER 2

The Treaty of Rome – Blueprint for a Wider Community

What sort of treaty is the Treaty of Rome? Unlike most previous treaties, it is not setting up a coalition to fight a war or a settlement concluding a war. It is different in kind, being instead the coming together of the signatories (the Member States), voluntarily, and the agreeing of several fundamental principles that will guide their actions and which the Member States, again voluntarily, agree to abide by. It is an *enabling* treaty, that creates the institutions and grants the powers to those institutions which ensure that the agreed aims of the signatories are carried out. Also, rather confusingly, what we know as the European Community was originally technically known as the European Communi*ties*, because it consisted of the European Coal and Steel Community, the European Economic Community and the European Atomic Energy Community. These theoretically (in fact they were the same but wearing different caps depending on which Community they represented) had different Councils, Commissions and Parliaments and operated separate budgets. (Their titles were different in the ECSC: the 'Special Council of Ministers' for the Council and the 'High Authority' for the Commission; the European Parliament was known as the 'Assembly'.) Under the 'Treaty establishing a Single Council and a Single Commission of the European

Communities' – known as the 'Merger Treaty' – signed in Brussels in April 1965, these theoretically separate parallel institutions were merged.

While the ECSC began to establish common European policies for two industries, laid down ideals to drive those policies that are more widely applicable, and founded the institutions whose role was to develop and govern the realisation of such policies, it nonetheless was a limited initiative, even if the steel and coal industries are important to national economies – though of course that importance has declined progressively in the last fifty years. All this changed after a meeting of the foreign ministers of the six ECSC members at the Messina conference, which led to the signing of the Treaty of Rome in March 1957, where the goals were much more ambitious. Instead of locking European nations together through the industries that historically provided the material for warfare, the aim was to make them economically interdependent in all fields of commerce, through a common market. The ECSC had been seen by its architects as the first step in a gradual process – one which is still continuing – of binding the nations of Europe together. Given how different from each other the economies of Europe were forty years ago, the idea of a common market was a quite visionary concept: West Germany, Italy and France were still recovering from the war, while the United Kingdom, not then a Member State, still regarded the United States and the Commonwealth as its natural trading partners. Exchange rates were fixed and exchange controls were the norm – for many years British tourists were only allowed a maximum of £30 of foreign currency, which in the 1960s was generously increased to £50! The free flows of money and goods which we now take for granted were not even conceived of.

THE TREATY OF ROME – THE EUROPEAN ECONOMIC COMMUNITY

The goals of the nations that signed the Treaty of Rome are best expressed in the words of the Treaty. Article 2 states:

The Community shall have as its task, by establishing a common market and progressively approximating the economic policies of Member States, to promote throughout the Community a harmonious development of economic activities, a continuous and balanced expansion, an increase in stability, an accelerated raising of the standard of living and closer relations between the States belonging to it.

'Approximating the economic policies' means making the economies of Member States more similar in terms of tax and excise regimes, social security provisions, distribution of income etc., so as to ensure a fair competitive environment. (If a company pays the same taxes and social security in one state as another, it will make decisions as to where to operate on purely commercial grounds, without being biased by tax incentives or disincentives.) VAT is a concrete example of the approximation of economic policies: all states in the EU operate VAT rather than other forms of sales tax. In the United Kingdom previously there was simply Purchase Tax, levied on the final sale of a good or service: VAT is added at each stage of a good's processing, being charged by the manufacturer to the distributor on his or her sale price, by the distributor to the retailer likewise, and finally by the retailer to the customer. VAT is charged at up to three rates – higher, standard and reduced. Higher tends to be applied to luxury items, as with luxury taxes in the past; standard has had to be above 15 per cent in the EU since 1 January 1993; and the reduced rate is usually for items like food, children's clothes and books and can be as little as zero, which it is in the United Kingdom, though the United Kingdom is under some pressure to put a positive rate on these types of item. Sales taxes are indirect taxes, i.e. everybody, however rich or poor, pays the same tax on any good or service they purchase, whereas direct taxes are such things as income tax or social security payments which are calculated on the basis of a person's income. VAT, as an indirect tax, was chosen as the first tax to be approximated because it is seen as having no effect on competition; a German product sold in France will attract 20 per cent VAT at the point of sale, while if it is sold in the United Kingdom it will attract 17.5 per cent

VAT, as would a product made in France. Thus consumers should not have their choices driven by tax differences. Where neighbouring Member States have different VAT rates this can still affect consumer choice, which is why the rate of 15 per cent was set; Germany and Spain were lower before 1 January 1993 at 14 and 12 per cent respectively. France initially tried to bring its standard rate down, but in August 1995 felt it necessary to increase the standard rate to 20.5 per cent. The rationale for this approach is that even if national governments alter their rates of direct taxation (a prerogative they jealously preserve), which does alter the basket of goods that consumers purchase – higher direct taxes lead to a decline in demand for such items as luxuries, new cars, TVs, hi-fis, etc. – nonetheless within the basket of goods that they do purchase, non-domestically produced goods are not discriminated against on a tax basis.

When the Treaty was signed, it was generally believed that the natural state of economies was one of a growth in prosperity: the aim was to encourage this, in the belief that growth would mean extra wealth for all citizens of the Community. For many years this was true, and the Community achieved high rates of growth – much higher than those of the United Kingdom, which is one of the reasons why the United Kingdom became keener on joining. But first of all the oil shock of 1973 put a brake on and even reversed growth. Growth was not spread evenly among EC members, with the per capita wealth of the rich countries growing more quickly than that of the poor, though Spain put on a spurt after its accession in 1986, and more recently Ireland has been showing a very high rate of growth at around 5 per cent in the last two or three years. More recently, too, especially in economies such as the United Kingdom, the growth in wealth has not been evenly distributed. Figures show that the extra wealth acquired through growth is largely going to the richer parts of the population, both within Member States and between Member States; the poorer nations are not catching up with the richer. The notorious Reaganite 'trickle-down' theory has guided some countries away from the original aims of the Treaty. Thus the aim of ensuring political stability through ensuring growing prosperity for the whole populace has not been achieved; although some progress was made initially, this is no longer the case and if anything it is being reversed.

Article 3 sets out in unambiguous language the aims of the EEC:

> For the purposes set out in Article 2, the activities of the Community shall include, as provided in this Treaty and in accordance with the timetable set out therein:
>
> (a) the elimination, as between Member States, of customs duties and of quantitative restrictions on the import and export of goods, and of all other measures having equivalent effect;
>
> (b) the establishment of a common customs tariff and of a common commercial policy towards third countries;
>
> (c) the abolition, as between Member States, of obstacles to freedom of movement for persons, services and capital;
>
> (d) the adoption of a common policy in the sphere of agriculture;
>
> (e) the adoption of a common policy in the sphere of transport;
>
> (f) the institution of a system ensuring that competition in the common market is not distorted;
>
> (g) the application of procedures by which the economic policies of Member States can be co-ordinated and disequilibria in their balances of payments remedied;
>
> (h) the approximation of the laws of Member States to the extent required for the proper function of the common market;
>
> (i) the creation of a European Social Fund in order to improve employment opportunities for workers and to contribute to the raising of their standard of living;
>
> (j) the establishment of a European Investment Bank to facilitate the economic expansion of the Community by opening up fresh resources;
>
> (k) the association of the overseas countries and territories in order to increase trade and to promote jointly economic and social development.

Member States agreed to make every effort to carry out the provisions of the Treaty and not to discriminate in any area where the Treaty was concerned on grounds of nationality, and they certainly held to the first part of this. The timetable for the removal of quotas and tariff barriers within the EEC, and the establishment of the Common External Tariff, was twelve years from the date of signing, and this was completed eighteen months ahead of schedule, one of the EU's great successes. Notably though, the provisions concerning freedom of workers to travel, as an aim, was now applied to all workers rather than just those in the coal and steel industries. There have been difficulties over fulfilling this aim, due to differing national legislation over professional qualifications. The obvious examples are doctors and lawyers; in the former case every nation would want to ensure that its own minimum standards are met, and in the latter quite different systems pertain – Roman law being the foundation of most law on the Continent, and common law the foundation in the United Kingdom. But engineers, builders, accountants and countless other vocations train to different levels under the various national legislations and the problem of recognition or standardisation is still with us, though steps are being taken to ameliorate this (see Chapter 5, 'Mutual recognition'), and part of the purpose of the Single European Act was specifically to address these delays. Statistics on the migration of labour are hard to come by, but large numbers of EU citizens work in the City of London in the international banking and finance industries, and at the other end of the income scale many British construction workers worked in Germany. As with so much EU legislation, though, it is difficult to ascribe the result, i.e. movement of workers, to the legislation or to other economic factors. Germany has also sucked in a large number of other nationals, Turks and citizens of ex-Yugoslavia (before the refugee crisis caused by the civil war). Also, the City employs many non-EU citizens. There is no doubt, though, that the status of EU citizen reduces the bureaucratic difficulties of seeking employment.

The role of the Commission in trying to minimise the problems caused by the restructuring of industry under the ECSC was institutionalised by the creation of the European Social Fund, in clause (i) above, and was now applicable in all industries. This interventionary role, supplementing national welfare schemes which do not necessarily take the larger view, as different industries fade or become more prominent globally, has been expanded with each new addition to the Treaty. The Single European Act has extended the process. The establishment of the European Investment Bank also indicated that the Community intended to marshal resources at its centre so as to reduce disparities between poorer and richer regions in the Community. The Structural Funds were created by the Treaty of Rome so as to further this process – the European Investment Bank might be described as primarily project-defined, i.e. its role is to support worthwhile projects, while the Structural Funds give broader regional aid, where essentially it is the regions themselves that choose projects to which to allocate funding.

Clause 9 specifies that the Community is based on a customs union, where no customs duties shall be levied on any goods originating within Member States and, importantly, once a good has entered the Community from a third country, having complied with import formalities – the Community also agreed a common external tariff – it shall be able to freely circulate. This clause is an important influence in encouraging inward investment – Japanese car or TV manufacturing in Derby and Bridgend, for example – as it gives Toyota and Sony access to the whole European market, even if the external tariff or quota walls were to be raised (the 'Fortress Europe' scenario). The United Kingdom has benefited from this, partly due to the fact that English is more familiar to the Japanese than other European languages, and partly due to the tax inducements granted by the Thatcher government to encourage inward investment, and anti-trades union legislation enacted to make British labour more attractive to outside investors. This has caused much dissension – both with our European partners and within the United Kingdom – though this has lessened as more external investment has been received by other Member States. Our European partners are concerned that the United Kingdom is using its labour legislation and welfare and unemployment provision to undercut its competition, basically by not affording the same rights to workers. Within the United Kingdom this also raises concern, as there is a feeling that the UK is becoming a Third World country with the disappearance of minimum wages as set by the Wages Councils from those industries in which they had operated, and the reappearance of the 'sweatshop'. (These concerns are often synthesised in the well-known 'poverty trap'.) The other concern, within both the United Kingdom and the rest of Europe, is that much inward investment is into 'screwdriver' plants which involve only a minimum of local expertise; the workforce simply assembles components imported by the inward investor. This is a cause for concern because pure assembly reduces the requirement for nationally based research and development and hence the need for highly trained and well-educated professional staff; i.e. industry in the United Kingdom becomes semi-skilled at best and we lose the capacity to stay at the forefront of technological innovation; and outside the United Kingdom the concern is that this effect will spread, as Japanese or Korean firms based in the UK drive their competitor industries in Europe out of business.

The Commission was also directed to reduce formalities imposed on trade (Clause 10.2), though in some respects it failed to do this over the years; for example, paperwork at borders was not reduced at internal borders until the introduction of the Single Administrative Document on 1 January 1988. This replaced the seventy forms previously used (and has now itself been abolished except when goods cross a third-country border). The sight of convoys of trucks tailing back from border posts as customs officials ground through reams of documentation had been common, even in the free market. There may have been no financial duty to pay on the goods transported, but there was a cost imposed by this delay. However the Single European Act (SEA, of which more later) has largely disposed of these problems; the SEA is what lies behind the well-known 1992 initiative (though in fact it should more properly be called the 1993 initiative as the deadline for completion was 31 December 1992). The Schengen Convention signed in June 1990, despite temporary French withdrawal (it requested a six-month extension of border-control maintenance in July 1995, and may request further extensions given the recent bomb attacks in France by Islamic fundamentalists) due to fears over security at external borders, and some squabbling over the stringency of drug controls, has augmented this by further reducing internal formalities while strengthening external ones. To the ordinary traveller going between say Belgium and France or France and Germany, border controls have appeared virtually non-functioning for several years.

The only exceptions to the abolition of tariffs and quotas within the internal market are where health and safety issues are involved or where national public policy differs (for example, children's toys produced in some countries have not always met United Kingdom standards, and the United Kingdom has the right to refuse them access to its market). The Community also specifically recognised that customs duties were a source of income and authorised countries to substitute alternative tax measures for this loss.

Finally, Article 29 details the principles by which the Commission should be guided:

In carrying out the tasks entrusted to it under this Section the Commission shall be guided by:
(a) the need to promote trade between Member States and third countries;
(b) developments in conditions of competition within the Community in so far as they lead to an improvement in the competitive capacity of undertakings;
(c) the requirements of the Community as regards the supply of raw materials and semi-finished goods; in this connection the Commission shall take care to avoid distorting conditions of competition between Member States in respect of finished goods;
(d) the need to avoid serious disturbances in the economies of Member States and to ensure rational development of production and an expansion of consumption within the Community.

Clause (a) is self-explanatory, but important. It is often forgotten that the EU looks outwards and it has signed many trade agreements, notably the Lomé Conventions (first signed in 1975) which give open access to the EU to ACP (Afro-Caribbean-Pacific) countries, but also with the EFTA (European Free Trade Association) countries (Switzerland, Norway and Iceland); the last two are now part of the European Economic Area, a free-trade zone including EU and EFTA countries, with a population of just under 400 million. The EEA was initially envisaged as a staging post for the accession of EFTA countries into the EU. However, Norway rejected EU membership in a referendum in 1994, and because a Swiss referendum rejected membership of the EEA Switzerland withdrew its EU membership application. The Commission has also dealt with the GATT (General Agreement on Tariffs and Trade) negotiations. Clause (b) is there because of an awareness that global economic competition is growing fiercer, and requires that EU countries and industries should be helped in every way to meet this threat. Clause (c) is to ensure that all Member States have equal access to materials; this developed partly because during the period of reconstruction in West Germany after the Second World War, France was threatened with a coal shortage as German industry began to consume a greater proportion of the coal it produced. The ECSC gave French and German industries equal access to German coal. Clause (c) applies this principle to all raw materials. Clause (d) is also an expansion of the Treaty of Paris provisions. It applies to the right of the Commission to intervene where Member States are subsidising particular industries, as originally happened to a large extent with steel and coal, and is still the case with the airlines, computers and other national 'flagship' industries.

THE 'FOUR FREEDOMS' – FREEDOM OF MOVEMENT FOR GOODS, PEOPLE, SERVICES AND CAPITAL

The original declaration in the Treaty of Paris (ECSC), that steel and coal workers should be able to move around the European Coal and Steel Community without hindrance, was extended in the Treaty of Rome to cover all workers. 'Freedom of movement for workers shall be secured within the Community . . .' These provisions have been further expanded in the Maastricht Treaty, but there are problems in carrying them out: notably, different national legislation for different professions and qualifications and, of course, language, which is in many ways the harder barrier to overcome. Initially, as with the adoption of other standards, the EC considered that the best approach would be to pass some overriding Community-wide legislation to supersede national legislation for each individual standard. However, when this process began the Commission soon became aware that such a harmonisation process would take decades, if not centuries, to complete. From this developed the idea of 'mutual recognition' (see Chapter 5, 'Mutual recognition') which, simply put, states that the national standards and qualifications of one state shall be deemed sufficient for any other Member States. The idea of mutual recognition has also been applied to vocational qualifications as well as goods. Two concerns are addressed in the Treaty: first that general qualifications are above an acceptable minimum in all states, and second that the qualifications accord with public policy within the Member State where a particular person might be seeking employment. A solicitor qualified in England or Wales would find the law substantially different in France or Spain, and would require some re-education (just as he or she would do if moving from contract law to divorce law within England or Wales), whereas a doctor's qualifications should prove universally applicable (in spite of the penchants of different nations for different types of ailment and different types of panacea), as should those of a builder or civil engineer. Citizens of the EU have the right to reside in the Member State where they have found employment and, where relevant, to stay in that state after a particular employment has ceased.

The contracting Member States also agreed that there should be co-operation between national employment services to ensure that job seekers in one part of the Union were made aware of suitable vacancies in another; *Eures*, a register of employment opportunities, is published and can be accessed via the Department of Employment in the United Kingdom. However, take-up is low and linguistic difficulties will persist for the foreseeable future, which is one of the reasons why the EU has taken positive steps to ensure that young people in particular have the opportunity to visit and study in other Member States; later generations should find language less of a barrier, especially if a *lingua franca* or a small number of *linguae francae* can be established. Several programmes are operated – Youth for Europe (projects for young people in general), Socrates (exchange programmes for young people and university students) and Leonardo (developing links between educational establishments and industry and promoting language training). The EU had spent ECU 287 million on these projects by the end of 1994.

Periods of qualification for employment by residence were abolished over time, and workers who are not citizens of a particular Member State are entitled to the same rights and conditions as those of that Member State. The Treaty also stated that the Council would ensure that citizens of the Union would, when in any Member State, be entitled to benefits as accorded by that Member State to its own nationals, with such benefits being portable, so to speak, across borders. (Thus, if one was entitled to ten weeks of accumulated benefit in country X, one should be able to claim for ten weeks in country Y.) Not unnaturally, this has led to some complaints, with richer countries accusing poorer ones of exporting their unemployment and claims of 'Euro-scroungers' in the British press. Migrant dole-chasing is not as easy as it sounds, though; for a start one needs to reach the country where one wants to claim unemployment benefit or income support (or however it is described). One then needs a fixed or permanent address, and finally has to go through the bureaucracy of claiming. From the United Kingdom's point of view, while there may be a small population of such dole-claimers it is hard to see why they have not headed for Germany, France, Holland, Denmark or Sweden, where the so-called 'pickings' are generally higher. And if a citizen employee from another Member State works here and is made unemployed, then their entitlement through the payment of United Kingdom taxes, quite apart from any taxes paid in their country of origin, should in natural justice entitle them to the same rights as other taxpayers. The purpose behind the co-ordination of the social security net is quite simple. It is to ensure that true freedom of movement is available for EU

citizens without their feeling restricted by the absence of entitle-
ments they would enjoy in their own countries of origin.

Rights of Establishment

In line with freedom of movement is the right of EU citizens to
establish themselves anywhere in the EU, either as a self-employed
person or by setting up companies or firms. In the original Treaty
of Rome, this was subject to restrictions on capital movements –
1992 was still a long way away, and some of these restrictions are
still in place for Portugal and Greece. As a general rule countries,
like individuals – and this does not just apply to EU countries – are
happy to see inward investment but can be reluctant to see the
remission of profits or the transfer of capital elsewhere. Countries
which feel secure with regard to the net inflow being larger than
the net outflow of funds i.e. those with strong economies, are
usually louder in their trumpeting of the virtues of free capital
movements.

The Commission's role was to propose measures to the Council
that would lead to the 'progressive co-ordination of the exchange
policies of Member States in respect of the movement of capital
between those states', with measures being taken to protect the
weaker countries – Ireland, Portugal, Spain and Greece.

The Treaty also provides that companies have the same rights
as individuals, and that third-country companies (i.e. those
primarily based outside the EU), once established within the EU
have the same rights as EU companies. This is what lay behind the
rush before 1992 of Japanese companies, in particular, to get a
foothold in the EU, primarily though not entirely in the United
Kingdom. EU companies are also investing across borders, though
this has much to do with global trends in industry, as large
commodity services (e.g. insurance and utility companies) and
large commodity product companies (from chemicals to computers) agglomerate and seek larger homogenised markets and
economies of scale. Also, in almost all areas of business countries
have developed particular areas of expertise – whether it be the
United Kingdom in financial services and privatised telecommunications, Germany in automobiles or France in water utilities – and
there is a certain inexorability to the fitter companies snapping up

their weaker counterparts in other EU countries. There is a constant tension between the desire to preserve one's own nation's presence in certain industries and the drive for greater efficiency, fuelled by increasing global competition. And in a certain sense there is an irony here, as global needs for openness outpace the ideal framework of legislative openness which the EU promotes and individual nations try to retard. Importantly, though, the EU – under its mutual recognition legislation – has now established that where a company has a licence in one EU state, that licence is valid in all EU states. This particularly affects service organisations (e.g. finance, travel agencies, advertising, PR etc.) and cuts much bureaucracy at a stroke. It is also true, as in the case of German or Dutch banks buying up British banks – Deutsche Bank has bought Morgan Grenfell, Dresdner Bank has bought Kleinwort Bensons, ING bought Barings after the Leeson disaster – that its more liberal regulatory framework makes the United Kingdom an attractive base from which to operate, and buying local firms provides some instant expertise which can then be absorbed by the purchaser. So, within the internal market decisions are still driven by regulatory differences.

Article 220 summarises the efforts that are expected, and the goals to be achieved with regard to freedom of movement:

Member States shall, so far as is necessary, enter into negotiations with each other with a view to securing for the benefit of their nationals:

— the protection of persons and the enjoyment and protection of rights under the same conditions as those accorded by each State to its own nationals;

— the abolition of double taxation within the Community;

— the mutual recognition of companies or firms within the meaning of the 2nd paragraph of Article 48 [the first clause under the Title III – 'Free movement of persons, services and capital'], the retention of legal personality in the event of transfer of their seat from one country to another, and the possibility of mergers between companies or firms governed by the laws of different countries;

— the simplification of formalities governing the reciprocal recognition and enforcement of judgements of courts or tribunals and of arbitration awards.

The only exception to this is that Member States do not have to reveal or exchange information that affects their security or any arms' trade interests.

NEW MEMBERS

Any European state can apply to join the EU. In the first instance it applies to the Council, which must agree unanimously after consulting the Commission and receiving a majority in favour from the European Parliament. Since this was agreed, Austria, Sweden and Finland have joined the EU, with Norway and Switzerland staying out. Both countries fear that EU membership will compromise their neutrality and that they will be net contributors. In addition Norway has fears about its fishing quotas. The states of Eastern Europe, Poland, the Czech Republic, Bulgaria and Rumania, Slovenia, Slovakia and Hungary would all like to join, as would some smaller entities such as Malta and Cyprus. 'Association' agreements were signed with Czechoslovakia, Poland and Hungary in 1991, with the expectation of free trade between these countries and the EU being established within a decade. Applicant states have to meet certain criteria regarding democracy and human rights legislation (and observance of such legislation), which last have made Turkey's entrance as a new member difficult. Greece is also unenthusiastic about Turkey's accession for historical reasons, and would be likely to veto any application. With regard to small states such as Malta and Cyprus which have also applied to join: it is quite difficult to see how these states would be represented in the Council and the Commission, and with Cyprus there is still the vexed question of its division into two halves.

CHAPTER 3

Treaty of Rome – Main Policy Planks

Over the years, the EU has constantly added to the areas of economic and social life in which it feels it has competence. It started with the ECSC as the means of restructuring the coal and steel industries, and then expanded this remit with the Treaty of Rome to cover agriculture – still in 1957 a major industry, certainly in terms of numbers employed – transport, the common market and other issues. Since then, the Maastricht Treaty has broadened the EU's remit.

COMMON AGRICULTURAL POLICY

The CAP – the Common Agricultural Policy – is the first thing one thinks of when the European Community and agriculture are mentioned in the same breath. The CAP has been one of the most contentious aspects of the development of the EC and the EU, and is a ready stick for politicians who wish to beat the whole idea of European integration. There is no doubt that the CAP does account for a high percentage of the EU budget (49.3 per cent in 1994), nor is there any question that the unscrupulous have taken advantage of the agricultural budget throughout the EU. There was a period when Irish farmers found it worth their while to export cattle to Northern Ireland, pick up an export premium (a bonus paid by the CAP to exporters), drive the cattle back and repeat the process. Belgians did the same over the Dutch border. Italians claimed subsidies for olive groves on land which had already been developed, satellite verification of claims not being anticipated by the dubious characters sending in their subsidy applications to Brussels. Other idiocies abound: the uprooting of one kind of crop to replace it with the latest subsidy-rich alternative, the butter and beef mountains, the wine lakes and set-aside. Also the agricultural and fishing sectors of the various economies have sometimes found it difficult to abide by EU laws on free trade – witness French farmers burning British lambs, or the arguments between Cornish and Spanish fishermen.

But it should be remembered that when the CAP was conceived, agriculture was not the superabundant provider that we now regard it as being. We would find it disconcerting, to say the least, to go to a baker now and be told that we could have one loaf for the week. But throughout the Second World War most of the population of Europe was on short rations, and the goal of making Europe self-sufficient in more than just its basic needs influenced the policy-makers. Further, the process of rural depopulation had begun, with peasants everywhere moving to the towns and cities in search of work. Part of the idea behind the CAP was to encourage those who lived and worked the land to stay there so as to ensure that strategic food requirements could always be met. Now the desire is to keep people on the land to preserve the environment and because rural migration to cities in search of work is simply exacerbating urban social problems since urban unemployment is already high. To do this it was felt that two things were necessary: farmers should receive an adequate income and they should be protected from the vagaries of price, depending on glut or shortage, that had constantly threatened their wealth. The agricultural sector of France *and* of much of Germany, and the Mediterranean Member States, is characterised by many tiny farms, barely more than peasant small-holdings. Conversely, agriculture in the United Kingdom is characterised by many fewer but larger farms, generally highly mechanised and relatively efficient. This led to some strife, as the United Kingdom felt its efficient farmers were being penalised to benefit farmers on the Continent, and that the United Kingdom was paying an unduly high price to support its Continental competition. However, it should not be forgotten that British farmers, including the large efficient holdings, also received the relevant subsidies and some grew rich as a result.

The articles in the Treaty of Rome defining agriculture are all-embracing:

'Agricultural products' means the products of the soil, of stockfarming and of fisheries and products of first-stage processing directly relating to these products.

The responsibilities of Member States are clearly defined:

The operation and development of the common market for agricultural products *must* [author's italics] be accompanied by the establishment of a common agricultural policy among the Members States.

The aims of the policy are clearly set out in Article 39 of the Treaty:

1. the objectives of the common agricultural policy shall be:
   (a) to increase agricultural productivity by promoting technical progress and by ensuring the rational development of agricultural production and the optimum utilisation of the factors of production, in particular labour;
   (b) thus to ensure a fair standard of living for the agricultural community, in particular by increasing the individual earnings of persons engaged in agriculture;
   (c) to stabilise markets;
   (d) to assure the availability of supplies;
   (e) to ensure that supplies reach consumers at reasonable prices.

It is quite bald in its intention to increase 'the individual earnings of persons engaged in agriculture' and in trying to even out market cycles, but the intent as expressed in clause (a) was to develop the technical efficiency of the agricultural sector. This has happened, but not in the broad sense anticipated. Agro-chemical businesses have flourished, but their market consists of the larger, more efficient farmers who can afford their products, and productivity has increased but, as mentioned in the introduction to this chapter, not necessarily in the most effective ways – intensive farming has led to fears over chemical residues and complaint about blander produce. Even though Article 41 states that part of the aim shall be 'joint measures to promote consumption of certain products', it was impossible that such consumption could absorb the enormously increased output of some subsidy-favoured items (production grew by 2 per cent per annum, consumption by 0.5 per cent); and much of the butter and beef mountains ended up being sold at highly subsidised prices to Russia, while the EU taxpayer footed the bill.

The means of carrying out the policy are detailed in Article 40, clause 2:

In order to attain the objectives set out in Article 39 a common organisation of agricultural markets shall be established.

This organisation shall take one of the following forms, depending on the product concerned:
(a) common rules on competition;
(b) compulsory coordination of the various national market organisations;
(c) a European market organisation.

The whole policy was to be based on common rules with funds being made available for agricultural 'guidance and guarantee'.

Whereas most states would agree on sub-clause (a), they find (b) and (c) less appealing, because of the degree of interference with national policy that they entail. Farming lobbies are strong out of proportion to their size and value to the economy. In France, often cited as being one of the states most influenced by the agricultural sector, the proportion of those employed in agriculture has fallen dramatically – from 7.9 per cent to 5.9 per cent – over the last decade, and in the United Kingdom the National Farmers' Union has close links with the Conservative Party.

There is a conservative sentimentalism with regard to the agricultural sector in many countries. Urbanising populations are nostalgic, especially where they have recently ceased to work in agriculture, and this sentimentality is converted into votes and hence disproportionate power by the farming lobby. One of the ways in which farmers use this power is to promote nationalistic attitudes with regard to agriculture, and thus where they disagree with Community policy they are often able to flout it. Where there are disputes about obeying European Union rules the farmers often simply disobey them, leaving their national governments (i.e. their taxpayers) to pay fines and/or compensation when the matter reaches the European Court.

Where the EU has managed to co-ordinate agricultural policy this has led to rows too with the United States, each side accusing the other of subsidising certain products. In addition, there are doubts about policies that lead to overproduction (and the notorious 'set-aside', where farmers are paid *not* to use land they had previously used) both because of its intrinsic wastefulness and because the export of surplus production at subsidised prices hits the agricultural producers of less-developed nations, both within and without Europe. The newly democratised countries of Eastern Europe would like to export more to the EU, and agricultural produce is one of the areas where they are competitive (though this is also changing for other industries – Fiat has invested heavily in Poland where the Cinquecento is produced, and Volkswagen was invited to take over Skoda in the Czech Republic). In theory, the EU claims it wishes to support these changed political entities and would be doing so by opening its market to their produce, but it has been sluggish in this respect – partly because of existing internal overproduction and partly because of the farming lobbies. Given that this goes against the benefit of consumers, clause (e) of the aims set out in Article 39, it can be seen that an internal contradiction has developed. The interests of farmers, consumers and taxpayers are at odds, and while steps are being taken to redress this it is a slow process.

Article 40 barely mentions at the end the 'agricultural "guidance and guarantee" fund' but this lies at the heart of the conflict. This innocuous phrase is the origin of a budget that has grown and grown, and which undoubtedly increased the cost of British entry into the EEC (as it then was). Even now, the CAP is estimated to cost a family of four over £10 per week. The purpose of 'guidance' is to help restructure the agricultural sector and 'guarantee' is price support. The guarantee element was to ensure that EU farmers received fixed prices, set annually by the Council of Ministers for each major product. Where they produced a surplus this was bought up by intervention agencies, and where prices fell below the agreed floor the CAP intervenes to support them. (As a generalisation, world prices have almost invariably been lower than EU prices, though with the switch of China from being a net grain exporter to an importer this may well change.) Where imports were cheaper than EU produce, levies were imposed to bring them up to EU price levels. Set-aside has proved something of a joke, with farmers quite predictably setting aside their least productive land and sometimes fraudulently claiming for unfarmable areas.

Article 42 specifies that there will be aid to help less efficient areas. These policies run the risk of perpetuating inefficiency, but there are two ways in which such aid can be used. First it can be simply used to improve the efficiency of the inefficient area, which is a positive goal, but the second use is simply to maintain the inefficiency of the inefficient area, which is in direct contravention of its spirit. But if one takes into account non-economic costs, such as damage to the environment, the abandonment of inefficient areas would directly cause this – so where to draw the line?

The language of other articles is vague: minimum prices are permissible 'where applicable and where they will help speed up technical progress'. 'Where applicable' is open to virtually any interpretation. Finally, another bone of contention is that Community policy is specifically stated to supersede national policy, with the Commission being advised by the Economic and Social Committee in its enactment of policy.

Reforms have occurred to redress the absurdities – the milk lake, the beef and butter mountains, the wine lake which have all been reduced substantially over the last few years. In 1979 a 'co-responsibility levy' was imposed on dairy farmers who exceeded their quotas, whereby they had to contribute to storage of excess production. In 1988 it was agreed by the Council that CAP funding should not grow by more than 74 per cent of the growth in EU GNP, and 'stabilisers' were introduced whereby a producer exceeding a 'maximum guaranteed quantity' lost the subsidies that applied – for all their production. But these reforms soon proved inadequate in the face of collapsing demand from the former Soviet Union, and from the Middle East because of the Gulf War.

Steps are being taken to reduce the size of the CAP budget. In 1994, the CAP accounted for 49.3 per cent of the EC budget, at ECU 375 billion, as opposed to 58.4 per cent in 1988. Reform of the CAP was agreed by the Council of Ministers in May 1992, with provision being made for keeping people on the land, protecting the environment and directly aiding hard-pressed farmers. The United Kingdom's Ministry of Agriculture has recently proposed (July 1995) that all subsidies to farmers be cut and that they compete on the open world market. The only exceptions were to be subsidies for otherwise uneconomic hill-farming and preserving the rural environment, in the United Kingdom's case for such things as hedgerows.

Fraud, too, has risen up the agenda, as the EU becomes more aware what bad publicity it generates – the myth of a bloated bureaucracy, riddled with corruption, is hard to banish. For farm fraud there is even a freephone service (UK number 0800 963595). The Economic Intelligence Unit gives a figure for *known* cases of agricultural fraud as being ECU 700 million, which equates to 1 per cent of the Community budget. To ginger up the laxer states, the Commission now has the power to recover money from countries which have failed to control fraud, and expects to recover ECU 1.52 billion in this way. Italy's charge is ECU 799 million, the United Kingdom's is 31 million, which one might describe as a regrettable reinforcing of stereotypes.

Agricultural subsidies are an extremely thorny issue worldwide – accusations of unfair subsidy regularly fly across the Atlantic – as they distort competition on world markets. Moreover this has knock-on effects for developing countries which could compete successfully – and which *need* to export agricultural products, both because they often have little else to export and because many of them are in debt to the developed world. This debt cannot be repaid without exports and in itself is a brake on their development; debt servicing alone costs many developing countries more than their exports earn. They are stuck in a vicious circle which has manifested itself by their real impoverishment. These arguments were well aired during the Uruguay round of the GATT negotiations which began in 1985 and continued for a decade. Other nations subsidise their agricultural sector: Switzerland does so, and the Japanese massively subsidise their rice farmers – and these are only examples.

There are conflicting interests at work. Mass rural depopulation, which first began with the Industrial Revolution in the United Kingdom or Great Britain as it was then known, has increased from a trickle to a massive flow in many parts of the world over the last fifty years, as jobs move from the land to the city and agriculture grows more efficient and less labour-intensive. But cities cannot provide work for all the job-seekers. The megacities that are now growing (Mexico City is predicted to have 20 million inhabitants by 2015) offer their new citizens little more than squalor, poverty and disease. The rush of migrant workers to cities in China's new economic zones has led to the government actively seeking to keep country dwellers in the country. New incentives have to be provided to stay near the land; if the population is not to actively work *on* it, it must be provided with alternatives to stay *near* it.

Subsidies also provoke argument for another reason. Even if the consumer pays a lower price in the shops – and this is often not the case; after all, the price in the shop is usually a direct multiple of the price at the farm gate, and often as not this has a floor set on it (see p. 33) – he or she is still paying a higher price for food through higher taxes.

Further, if one allows the market free rein, then the old agricultural cycle will reassert itself. Naturally farmers, like the rest of humanity, seek to maximise their income. If in one year there is a scarcity of an agricultural product, the price will rise. Farmers not producing that product will tend to move into it the following year. The result: the price falls. How does one iron out these cycles? The easiest answer is central direction – but how is this most easily operated? Via subsidies? Subsidies, also, when directed at output (i.e. for farmers, they are subsidised for each unit of output) favour larger, more efficient producers, which is directly contrary to the purpose of the CAP.

Solutions to these problems – ensuring adequate food supplies, keeping people on the land, ensuring that farmers' incomes are not too vulnerable to the agricultural cycle, and keeping prices down for consumers – are immensely complex. The least expensive route, perhaps – direct income support for poor farmers – smacks too much of welfare and as such is resented by farmers, traditionally an independent breed, but now looks set to become the primary instrument of the CAP. Finally, it should perhaps be remembered that the CAP has in a sense been a victim of its own success. Production grew by 2 per cent a year until recently, whereas consumption was either static or grew at a maximum of 0.5 per cent. This in turn raises an ethical issue; EU food aid has been substantial, especially to Russia, and food aid is obviously a convenient means of disposing of surpluses. Reducing over-production is outwardly a laudable aim, but if one cuts surpluses in a world short of food, is that the most humane course?

TRANSPORT POLICY

The European Union's transport policy was intended to be one of the pillars of the Union's legal structure, alongside its agricultural policy. It is obvious that if one wants to economically unify a diverse geographical area, then smooth and efficient transport links will greatly assist. The Commission has direct responsibility for railways, roads and internal waterways, while air and sea links are left to the Council, both because they involve external issues and, in the case of air routes, because the processes of deregulation, allocation of routes, subsidies and so on are highly charged politically. National rail and road networks were until recently largely self-contained, so one would have anomalies like the rail service from Strasbourg being better to Paris than to Frankfurt (am-Main), which is much closer. Border crossings were intended as much to restrict as to encourage the flow of goods and people between countries, and links via border posts between national rail and road networks were not enthusiastically developed. It is true that the transport infrastructure of a nation has much to do with what it regards as its strategic interests (therein lies the origin of the autobahns in Germany) and historically much more attention has been paid to internal than external movement in transport planning. The current British delay in building the Chunnel link from the Channel Tunnel to London and beyond could be said to be a hangover of such archaic thinking, with the issue of whether it should be paid for out of public funds or private capital being a political red herring.

There are also other problems, especially with internationalising railway links between countries. While the TGV (Train à Grande Vitesse) has shrunk France, it is unable to expand its operations into Germany due to a differing loading gauge. Conversely the German high-speed ICE trains cannot operate in France as they use a different pantograph system (overhead power supply), and neither can operate in the United Kingdom again because the UK loading gauge (which determines platform heights, tunnel circumferences, bridge heights etc.) is smaller than those of its European counterparts. Road links are obviously easier to internationalise, and there is a European programme for the development of road links and also of classification; all major European roads now have an 'E' number, whichever country they are in. Road links also have problems though: with the growth of road transport, greater efficiencies have been sought by increasing the size of trucks, some of which are virtual road-trains. This means that bridges and road surfaces have to be brought up to international weight-bearing standards, which has imposed significant costs on countries with less developed road networks. (In the United Kingdom, for example, there was much resistance to the introduction of 40- and then 44-tonne lorries, both because of the increased infrastructure costs and because of likely environmental damage.) Anyone who has encountered a juggernaut down a country road at night, as its driver seeks to avoid motorway tolls and congestion, may feel that these efficiencies have their unpriced costs!

The Maastricht Treaty emphasised the creation of trans-European networks (TENs) which seek to join up European road and rail systems into a coherent whole, eliminating bottlenecks and giving better access to peripheral regions, and thereby making them more economically attractive. Current plans envisage many new cross-routes being developed (i.e. routes that ignore transport systems based on traditional national needs), with high-speed (250 kph or more) rail links being built. France has declared its aim of building 4,700 kilometres of high-speed track, of which over 700 kilometres have been completed. Only in the United Kingdom and Denmark will no such routes be built (apart from the still-unstarted Chunnel link to London); instead existing lines will be upgraded to a circa 200 kph level. The Commission is also keen to expand the use of combined road-rail transport, primarily to reduce pollution.

Recently, too, emphasis has been placed on TENs for energy transport, the two main aims being security of supply and the matching of deficits and surpluses of energies; for example, it is most efficient to run electricity plants at a constant level, but demand is by no means constant – the United Kingdom, for example, always suffers from major surges in demand throughout the advertisements during popular TV programmes as the nation rushes to its electric kettles – and this effectively means that to always have sufficient supply one always has to have surplus supply, which is clearly wasteful. Over a larger geographical area, though, the peaks and troughs in demand will tend to average out, which means the total amount of energy used can be lower, so the ability to switch supplies to different areas represents a significant saving. Trans-European gas pipeline networks would also guarantee supply. Europe's gas comes from the North Sea, Russia and Algeria, with Germany being more dependent on supplies from Russia and France from Algeria. The supply of gas to France and Germany could be cut off, depending on the political situation in the supplying countries, and a trans-European gas network would avert this possibility, at least until any political crises had resolved themselves.

One of the major issues involved in transport is 'cabotage', particularly for trucking and airline companies. Cabotage rules are imposed by national governments to protect their transport industries; airlines, for example, are often in the news as governments negotiate the allocation of landing slots, but other transport restrictions for trucking or coastal shipping are not newsworthy. Cabotage is the imposition of restrictions, often through licensing requirements, on the operational area of transport companies. For example, a minimal licence would allow one to operate one's trucks within 30 kilometres of a specified town, which essentially would enable one to be a localised delivery service. Anyone who wanted to transport goods beyond the 30-kilometre radius would have to acquire an additional licence at significant cost. And if, say, one moved goods from town A to town B, 40 kilometres away, one would not be allowed to pick up goods in town B to transport back to town A but would have to drive back empty. (Of course, if parts of one's organisation are in town B then one could perhaps take a load back, but this is a minor exception on the pan-European scale.) A truck with a 40-kilometre licence to operate from town B would be required to take goods from B to A. On the face of it this is an incredibly wasteful system, as a full truck B follows an empty truck A to the town of A before wending its lonely, unladen way back to B. Duplication is required both of the trucks themselves and of the fuel consumption. The only people this benefits are truck manufacturers and oil companies. Cabotage is enforced throughout Germany, which has resisted change, fearing that it will be swamped by cheaper-rate non-German trucks touting for business. On a European scale cabotage seems incredibly wasteful and hence expensive, ultimately for the consumer, given the enormous distances that are travelled. It is true that sometimes there is practical cabotage in the sense that car transporters taking Seats to Germany may have to return empty or partly empty since the reverse flow of cars from Germany to Spain is much smaller, and car transporters are role-specific. Cabotage remains an unresolved issue for ground transport.

For air transport very little progress in liberalisation has been made, with most countries jealously guarding rights of access to their internal markets. Consecutive cabotage is now allowed, whereby a flight originating in one country can pick up and fly passengers between two destinations in another, and full cabotage is supposed to be in place by 1997. Attempts to impose a common EU policy with third countries, specifically 'open skies' agreements with the United States, have failed, and the Transport Commissioner, Neil Kinnock, has seen individual countries (including Luxembourg – at how many airports can US airlines land there?) drawing up separate agreements. Many state airlines, such as Air France, are still heavily subsidised or mostly publicly owned, and true competition and deregulation is some way off. National political issues raise their heads here, and an attempt to slim down Air France failed in the face of widespread union protest.

Unlimited cabotage is now applied to shipping, with the exception of Greece, where restrictions will apply until 2004, and for some island services. For inland waterways – canals and rivers, which are extensively utilised on mainland Europe, though use is declining – cabotage has been operative since January 1993.

Another initiative which has been crowned with success is the Single Administrative Document, which replaced the plethora of documentation that formerly greeted truckers at frontiers.

In the event, despite its importance, transport has received far less attention than agriculture. Despite the recognition that the road network is reaching saturation in parts of the EU, and the Commission's plans to counter this (TENs), environmental issues are blocking development (in the United Kingdom, for example, plans for the proposed widening of the M25, the London orbital motorway, were dropped due to widespread opposition).

COMPETITION POLICY

The aim of the EU is to achieve a level playing field. Article 85 bans any price-fixing, either by seller or buyer, or any attempt to set up cartels to control markets. Solvay of Belgium and ICI were each fined ECU 7 million for operating a soda-ash cartel in 1990, though this was overturned by the European Court of Justice in 1995 on appeal; in other words there is a constant monitoring of industrial practices, but equally industry has the right to appeal Commission judgements. Also banned by Article 85 are discriminating between trading partners as to terms and conditions, or forcing unrelated supplementary agreements on trading partners before undertaking contracts. In March 1995 an association of Dutch building contractors was fined ECU 22.5 million by the

Court of Justice for breaking competition legislation.

Co-operation is allowed where this can be shown to be necessary to 'improving the production or distribution of goods or to promoting technical or economic progress, while allowing consumers a fair share of the resulting benefit'.

The abuse of monopoly power is dealt with in Article 86 and is prohibited; it should be remembered that a monopoly does not mean a sole company within a market, it means a company that dominates a market and such domination can mean the company controls as little as 25 per cent. Much company analysis has shown that to be the largest company within a market often enables one to set trends, of pricing or distribution or product development, for example, that one's competitors are obliged to follow if they wish to stay in business – hence the apparently small percentage needed to dominate.

The Treaty declares EU law to be supreme, and that Member States are not allowed to enact legislation that goes against the Treaty. Subsidies and dumping (the selling of goods at lower than cost) are banned, though there are certain exceptions with regard to subsidies, covered in Article 92. This includes: social payments, i.e. various forms of welfare, to individual consumers so long as they can use the aid to buy any products they like (rather than being forced to buy national); and aid in the case of 'natural disasters or exceptional occurrences'. The EU will exercise discretion over whether other forms of aid are permissible, according to circumstances: such as aid for depressed regions, aid granted towards projects of 'common European interest' and any other types of aid which the Council agrees by a qualified majority after a proposal by the Commission. It is the Commission's responsibility to ensure that other forms of aid are stopped, and either it or any other interested party can apply to the Court of Justice to achieve this. Nonetheless the Council can make exceptions and the Commission has to allow it three months to make decisions on particular exceptions; if it fails to do so within that period, then the Commission can go ahead.

Chapter 2 of 'Competition Policy', Articles 95–98, lays down that goods from all other Member States should pay no more tax than similar goods originating within the Member State where they are sold. VAT, which is the major sales tax in most countries, should be the same for each category of good, whatever their state of origin. In Article 99, the Council undertook to work towards the harmonisation of legislation affecting indirect taxes applied to goods and services, and to do so by 31 December 1992. (This part of the Treaty of Rome, as implied by the deadline, was amended by the Single European Act.) Much of this work was done, with over 90 per cent of directives being passed by the deadline. One important addition that began to emerge as being part of EU policy was the proviso in Article 100a that the Commission, when putting forward its proposals for the approximation of legislation 'concerning health, safety, environmental protection and consumer protection, will take as a base a high level of protection'.

Other amendments introduced by the SEA included agreement that each Member State would 'pursue the economic policy needed to ensure the equilibrium of its overall balance of payments and to maintain confidence in its currency, while taking care to ensure a high level of employment and a stable level of prices' (Article 104). Article 105 goes on to state that Member States 'shall co-ordinate their economic policies', so as to achieve the aims of 104. A Monetary Committee was set up to advise on achieving this, reporting to the Commission and providing opinions on request to the Council and the Commission. Member States and the Commission each appoint two members to the Committee.

These Articles lie behind the talk of economic convergence that is a preamble to the single currency, which is currently causing so much debate in the EU. The United Kingdom, in particular, has a group of right-wing Conservative MPs who oppose any notion of a single currency, declaring that financial union is the prologue to political union and involves a loss of sovereignty. Voices have also been raised in Germany, both involving the same issues and also the widespread fear of tying their strong currency to weaker ones such as sterling, the lira and the peseta (known as 'chocolate' currencies in Germany after the foil-wrapped coins!). The arguments in this field are bedevilled by jingoism and irrationality clouding the true issues. The forces against a single currency in the United Kingdom and France – the latter more so now under the right-leaning Chirac presidency – seem to regard sovereignty as a quantifiable national resource, rather as if one had a sovereignty 'bank' and could check one's sovereignty account on a quantifiable basis. But in this arena there are two kinds of sovereignty, political and economic. Absolute political sovereignty might be described as the ability to make decisions within one's own country that are totally unaffected by any actions by external forces and completely immune from outside interests. In short, it is an unattainable state, as an acquaintance with history will show, since the earliest times. We are left then with relative sovereignty. In the United Kingdom it is often argued that the greatest amount of relative sovereignty can be retained by the state if it turns its back on Europe and reverts to the relationships important fifty years ago – the so-called 'special relationship' with the United States and our ties with the Commonwealth – as if that were a unilateral decision we could make, as if political developments, the gradual division of the world into trading blocs – the EU itself, the Pacific Rim and the North American Free Trade Area (NAFTA) countries – could be ignored.

British political sovereignty, as defined by its ability to act under its own volition outside its geographical borders, has never recovered from the Suez Crisis of 1956, when the United States leaned on the United Kingdom and France and forced them to hurriedly withdraw from their Egyptian adventure. The Falklands adventure, relatively small as it was, was only possible with the assistance and approval of the United States, and our presence in the former Yugoslavia is under UN auspices. In other words, the freedom to act independently in the external political domain is extremely restricted. And in the internal political domain, within its borders, external political pressures circumscribe a government's freedom of action. The Brent Spar oil-rig disposal episode of summer 1995 is an example of this. Though the British government had given approval for Shell to sink the rig in the deep Atlantic (and environmental arguments over whether or not this was the best solution have not been properly resolved), German boycotting of Shell stations, where sales dropped significantly overnight, drove the company into changing its plans and making a mockery of British government policy. And the growing internationalisation of companies, though it might be thought to affect economic sovereignty primarily, also has many political ramifications. This internationalisation goes beyond EU borders. The Americans have long retained a European presence (Ford has been in Europe since 1929) and the Japanese have moved in. This means that decisions with pan-European effects can be taken in Detroit or Tokyo; these decisions may be affected by national policies on encouraging inward investment or by national employment laws or by national environmental standards, or whatever, but they are made from the viewpoint of Detroit and Tokyo, not Ghent or Saarlouis. Within the EU, cross-border mergers have become increasingly common, and these too diminish economic sovereignty. National governments have to respond to the concerns of industries whose actions are not determined by national considerations.

Fears for cultural sovereignty are also evident, both within the EU and outside it. Currently one of the major concerns is the domination of the European film market by American films, and the French have led the initiative to repel this invasion. The apparently unstoppable march of the hamburger has also raised blood pressure (probably literally as well), again particularly in the gourmet homeland. Quite unreal fears exist of Europroducts (the straight cucumber, for example – see Chapter 9, Euromyths) driving out local varieties. If British topers buy German, French, Dutch or Danish beer, they are not being unpatriotic or being conned by Europroducts; they are simply voting with their wallets and showing their preferences. (Some even buy American beer, but there is no explanation for this.)

Member States agreed in Article 107 to treat their exchange-rate policy as a matter of common concern. To most of us, travelling as tourists throughout Europe, we are only really aware of exchange rates when we go on holiday, and then the countries we visit seem surprisingly cheaper or more expensive than when we last visited. But for the larger economy, exchange rates matter (and change) on a minute-by-minute basis. France has pursued the so-called *franc fort* (strong franc) policy for several years now, keeping its currency closely in line with the deutschmark. The exchange-rate mechanism (ERM) initially required European currencies to remain within two bands (percentage points difference from the average), one of 2 per cent, one of 6 per cent (for the less stable currencies). The United Kingdom and Italy were unable to sustain this and dropped out in mid and late September 1992 respectively, and in 1995 Spain and Portugal dropped out of the broad band – Portugal largely having to follow Spain's lead because of its heavy dependence on the Spanish economy. The Dini government hoped to have Italy back in the ERM by October 1995, as inflation had dipped and the budget deficit had fallen; Theo Waigel, the German finance minister, in September 1995 expressed doubts that this would happen and these proved correct.

Foreign exchange

The maintenance of a stable exchange-rate regime is crucial to the creation of fair competition. While visiting Spain, Portugal, the United Kingdom or Italy has become relatively cheaper for the Dutch or Danish tourist, there has been a bonanza for Spanish agricultural exporters, and Fiat and other Italian companies have seen demand for their products boosted Europe-wide – but at the expense of enterprises in the strong-currency bloc (Germany, France, the Netherlands, Austria, Denmark, Sweden and Ireland). French agriculture has been particularly hard-hit, but also the *franc-fort* policy has limited the government's ability to run budget deficits (for example, to alleviate unemployment through large government projects), and caused social divisions – those who are employed and have money will find it is worth more in a European context, and of course they benefit from low national inflation, while those who are unemployed have almost nothing – and unemployment is always exacerbated by a strong currency as it makes exports less attractive (Jean Calvet of Peugeot has long argued for abandonment of the *franc-fort* policy, for these reasons). France has suffered particularly because it is next to two weak-currency nations, Spain and Italy, with which it trades extensively, and thus is highly exposed to their devaluations.

Alterations in exchange-rate policy have to receive the approval of the Commission, in consultation with the Monetary Committee. Member States are allowed to act independently in a crisis but have to keep the Commission informed and may find that the Council reverses measures they have taken. The Commission may recommend measures to the Council in the event of a Member State facing real balance-of-payment difficulties.

There is another issue involved in exchange-rate policy, and that is the sheer cost of transactions. Most of us have encountered the difference between a bank's 'buy' and 'sell' rates which can be substantial – up to 5 per cent (the banks themselves pay a much smaller 'spread' to buy and sell on the money markets), to which commission of up to 2 per cent is often added. Both the *Guardian* (1995) and the *Sunday Times* (1991), two British national newspapers, have conducted experiments, taking £100 with them and exchanging it in three or four countries. When they returned to the United Kingdom to swap their guilders or Belgian francs, both received about £65, a whacking 35 per cent loss! The idea of a common market has been described as a 'bankers' conspiracy' because, of course, the spread and the commission go into bankers' pockets, and if the EU wishes to really open the internal market it should do something to reduce these costs. The Commission ran a survey in 1995 which showed that many banks double-charged, in 36 per cent of cases charging a fee at both the sending and receiving ends, resulting in a net 16 per cent cost to transferers! Ironically, though, while the EU is now addressing these issues with a series of proposals, the march of technology is making much of the argument obsolete. Electronics make it as easy to withdraw cash in Troyes as in Tuebingen, in Toledo as Taranto. Strangely, with a wad of francs in one's hand, or marks or pesetas or lire, the design of the notes seems utterly irrelevant; what matters is: 'Will this particular type of paper work when you order a coffee in the local bar?' Electronics mean too that the credit or charge card has become an increasingly frequently used means of purchase, and even as this is being written the Mondex experiment is underway in Swindon, Britain, whereby a chargeable card is used to pay for such small-ticket items as newspapers (the first transaction amounted to 28p – about 2.30 FFr or 65 pfennigs, 54 pesetas, 700 lire). The EU itself is running a chip-card experiment with a card that stores value in several currencies as well as the ECU. When notes and coins are rapidly declining in total percentage value of transactions, arguments about names for a currency become increasingly irrelevant. The only area where electronics have not been put to real use is in reducing the cost to the consumer of transactions involving currency exchange, despite the fact that it is simple enough to calculate real exchange rates on a real-time basis – measured in seconds rather than minutes – and despite the huge savings which banks reap from moving cash electronically down phone lines rather than in armoured vans.

Another development in the cash realm is that because people know the value of their currency vis à vis other currencies they are increasingly willing to accept cash in other currencies, more so of course near border areas, where travel for work or pleasure across borders is frequent. Some Brussels taxi drivers accept French as well as Belgian francs, even if the exchange-rate they offer is not over-generous – but, then, when did a taxi ride seem cheap? If a driver had been offered Swedish krone, he would probably have awarded himself an equally handsome *pourboire*.

COMMERCIAL POLICY

This area has been of growing importance within the EU as the Commission has signed more and more trade agreements on behalf of EU Member States as mentioned earlier (see p. 22) in the discussion of the powers delegated to the Commission. The opening words of the chapter on commercial policy define the vision (Article 110):

> By establishing a customs union between themselves Member States aim to contribute, in the common interest, to the harmonious development of world trade, the progressive abolition of restrictions on international trade and the lowering of customs barriers.
>
> The common commercial policy shall take into account the favourable effect which the abolition of customs duties between Member States may have on the increase in the competitive strength of undertakings in those States.

Under the Treaty, EU countries have agreed to maintain a

common policy with regard to third countries and with international economic organisations. The Commission is authorised to act on their behalf when dealing with such bodies as the GATT (General Agreement on Tariffs and Trade), which recently completed the Uruguay round, though not without some last-minute nail-biting as France tried to establish a quota system for imported films (with the aim of reviving its domestic industry) and the United States responded with renewed complaints about EU agricultural subsidies. The Commission has also signed accords with the ACP countries and other groups. The course of action it takes is decided by the Council, acting by a qualified majority, based on proposals the Commission submits.

Article 113 specifies that:

> After the transitional period has ended, the common commercial policy shall be based on uniform principles ...

and this has been carried out by the Commission, with the result that third countries and international organisations think of the Commission as representing a unified Europe, at least in trade matters. For example, in the recent dispute with Canada over the exploitation of fishing grounds, Spain was effectively represented by the Commission, not its own government. The Maastricht Treaty amended this clause by dropping the reference to a transitional period, since by 1992 this was considered over.

Originally, in the event of a crisis, Member States could get retrospective permission from the Commission for measures they instituted; after the Maastricht Treaty they have to receive authorisation from the Commission first, which is to act as quickly as possible. The Commission can decide at any time that any such measures should be amended or abolished.

SOCIAL POLICY

This is another contentious issue within the Union. One of the noted tendencies of recent years is for Europeans to elect a majority of MEPs who hold opposite views to the majorities within their own parliaments and currently, contrary to the general swing to the

right in the national elections of the larger EU countries, the
Socialist group dominates within the European Parliament. The
Treaty contains what must be considered unexceptionable aims by
politicians of any colour, but it is in the interpretation that
arguments arise. Also it cannot be denied, certainly for the United
Kingdom, and probably elsewhere, that politicians tend to turn a
blind eye to agreed principles that their predecessors have subscribed to; Kenneth Clarke, currently the British Chancellor of the
Exchequer, famously declared that he had not read the Maastricht
Treaty, and he is considered a Europhile within the Tory Party –
though he is unlikely to try to renege on what the United Kingdom
has agreed to, unlike the Tory Europhobe wing which never seems
to have had a true idea as to what provisions Margaret Thatcher put
her name to as Prime Minister.

> Member States agree upon the *need* [author's italics] to
> promote improved working conditions and an improved
> standard of living for workers, so as to make possible their
> harmonisation while the improvement is being maintained.

This opening paragraph of the Title on Social Policy is quite
specific: it is the duty of Member States to work to this end. (The
second half of the sentence is not quite so clear: basically it is
saying that the EU should work to bring the living standards and
working conditions of its poorer workers up to a common high
standard, which itself is growing higher. The Greeks and the
Portuguese should expect to enjoy living standards and working
conditions similar to the Germans, the Dutch and the Lux-
embourgeois, even while those standards and conditions continue
to improve for the latter.)

The problems with this part of the Treaty have arisen because
of the inexorable rise of unemployment throughout most of the EU
over the last decade or so, especially among the young. Spain for
example has had unemployment of around 23–25 per cent for
several years now, and where unemployment is lower, as in
France (c. 12 per cent) and the United Kingdom (c. 8.5 per cent)
one suspects the true figures are much higher, since the governments of both countries run 'vocational' and other programmes

which technically remove the unemployed from the statistics. The effectiveness of these programmes is highly doubtful: there are rarely jobs available at the end of them, and frequently when they involve work experience (often subsidising employers to take on the young unemployed temporarily) they are seen both as cheap labour and a threat to other employees. Structural unemployment has been particularly hard to tackle – this is the sort of unemployment that often affects whole regions as a major industry, say shipbuilding or steelmaking, goes into terminal decline – and many who are structurally unemployed find it impossible to obtain jobs and remain permanently unemployed. It was partly to avoid this that the EU has been so keen on the idea of freedom of movement. Unfortunately, though, structural employment tends to cross borders; industries in decline often decline, albeit at slightly different rates, throughout a region. German and Swedish shipyards are as affected by Korean competition as British ones. Some industries have successfully restructured to face the growing competitive threat or a decline in demand or both, but usually restructuring requires a major diminution in the workforce. It has even been the case that new efficient plant, such as the Ravenscraig steel works in Scotland, has been closed shortly after completion, because of global trends in the demand for steel – though some would ascribe this particular closure to the fact that there are extremely few Conservative voters in Scotland. The other restraints on the freedom of movement of labour have been linguistic, and the resistance of trades unions to the employment of cheaper labour from other lower-wage Member States.

The rise in unemployment, in tandem with the slow-down in growth rates that has been with us since the oil crisis of 1973, has led Member States to question their commitment to (or their ability to fund) the social welfare states that seemed to have become the standard model after the Second World War in Europe, and consequently their commitment to the goals set out in the Treaty of Rome. This crisis is global, as indicated by the Group of Seven (G7) summit of December 1994, when unemployment pushed inflation off the head of the agenda.

The Commission's brief is clear though, set out in Article 118:

Without prejudice to the other provisions of this Treaty and in conformity with its general objectives, the Commission shall have the task of promoting close co-operation between Member States in the social field, particularly in matters relating to:
— employment;
— labour law and working conditions;
— basic and advanced vocational training;
— social security;
— prevention of occupational accidents and diseases;
— occupational hygiene;
— the right of association, and collective bargaining between employers and workers.

The Commission is advised by the Economic and Social Committee (see pp. 68–9 for composition).

Article 118a declares the importance of improving the health and safety of workers at workplaces, and establishing common EU standards. The Council is to act, by qualified majority, on proposals from the Commission which in turn co-operates with the European Parliament and the Economic and Social Committee, before issuing directives to establish these standards, with the important provisos that states which already have better employer protection than the EU standard can retain this, and that the establishment of an EU social policy framework should not impede (through extra bureaucracy) the creation and establishment of small and medium-sized businesses.

The principle of equal pay is also set out in Article 119:

Each Member State shall during the first stage ensure and subsequently maintain the application of the principle that men and women should receive equal pay for equal work.

This applies whether the work is piece-rate or hourly paid.

As is well known, this principle has not been fully implemented. Women are not equally represented in the professions, and many are paid less than their male equivalents. Very few women hold senior positions in commerce or politics (only 11 per cent of MPs in Europe were female in 1992). Legislation in areas such as child care and sexual harassment, for example, is still widely varied between Member States (the United Kingdom dislikes the idea of anything that will increase employers' costs, such as child care). Also, a large percentage of women are not in employment (55 per cent of women were employed in 1983, 60 per cent in 1990). With the ageing of the population, this is seen as a wasted resource, and even private enterprise has taken steps to make itself more attractive to potential female employees. Recently, in October 1995, the European Court of Justice ruled that positive discrimination (quotas) in favour of women applicants to positions went against the principle of equal rights: this was greeted with some consternation by women's groups throughout Europe. However, denying the right to positive discrimination is not the same as discriminating against, and technically means equality for both sexes. Also, it does not detract from ongoing efforts to help women to qualify for positions, especially in professions or vocations where they are poorly represented. In the longer term, this is what should produce true equality.

The Directorates-General for Employment, Industrial Relations and Social Affairs run the programme to redress this situation and have specified three areas of attack: equality at work; equal opportunities for training; and provision for child care. A network of training schemes (IRIS) has been set up, and the EU approves of affirmative action in that it recommends that where there are equally qualified candidates, male and female, positions should be given to women. It is also concerned that educational stereotypes (i.e. what are considered 'girls' subjects') should be abolished, particularly noting the low take-up of engineering by females.

It also has reservations about much of the new women's employment which has been created over the past few years, as it is aware that a kind of segregation is at work, with the new jobs being low paid 'women's work'. The United Kingdom textile industry is a classic example of this, with pay kept at very low levels. In tandem with this is the fact that many more women work part-time (28 per cent versus 4 per cent of men in 1991).

The European Social Fund (ESF) was also established, its task being to increase employment opportunities for and improve the geographical and occupational mobility of workers in Europe. (The Maastricht Treaty adds to this by specifying that it shall assist workers to adapt to industrial restructuring, especially through vocational training.) It is administered by the Commission with the assistance of a committee comprised of government, trades union and employers' representatives. The ESF originally provided up to 50 per cent of the cost of retraining or resettlement allowances, and of temporarily laying off workers if the undertakings they work for convert to different products; but under the Maastricht Treaty this limit became discretionary, and the Council now decides in conjunction with the Economic and Social Committee what financial support shall be provided. The Fund pays out grants only if those who have undergone vocational training for a new occupation or who have been resettled in a new area have been in full employment for six months – that is, once retraining has been shown to be successful and resettlement necessary.

ECONOMIC AND SOCIAL COHESION

'Economic and social cohesion' is the phrase applied to the long-term goal of the EU of bringing all its Member States up to a generally high standard of living, through redirecting resources from the richer to poorer states. It was added to the Treaty of Rome by the Single European Act, as it was felt that the EU should make a more positive contribution to the reduction in disparities between the per capita wealth of different states.

The EIB (the European Investment Bank) is one of the instruments of this policy, as are the so-called 'structural funds' – the European Agricultural Guidance and Guarantee Fund (subsumed under the CAP), the European Social Fund and the European Regional Development Fund (set up in 1975). Success in this field, as for unemployment, has been retarded by the decrease in the rate of growth of the rich Member States – and, of course, the expensive reunification of Germany – who have become less willing to supply the necessary funds, and who have demanded that more stringent controls be applied to EU spending. Article 130a clearly sets out the EU's objectives:

> In order to promote its overall harmonious development, the Community shall develop and pursue its actions leading to the strengthening of its economic and social cohesion.
>
> In particular the Community shall aim at reducing disparities between the various regions and the backwardness of the least-favoured regions.

The SEA specified that not only should recognisably poorer states be helped out – Portugal and Greece, for example – but that declining industrial regions in the richer states should also be eligible for EU aid, and this has certainly benefited the United Kingdom, France, Belgium and the northern regions of Finland.

RESEARCH AND TECHNOLOGY

As part of its expanding role as co-ordinator of European economic policy, the Member States agreed in the SEA that the EU should take an active role in overseeing research and technological development, running its own programmes and assisting Member States in theirs.

> The Community's aim shall be to strengthen the scientific and technological basis of European industry and to encourage it to become more competitive at [an] international level.

This is in part a reaction to the need to respond to global trends, where research and development is becoming an increasingly internationalised activity, due to the high cost of investment in new products whether they be aeroplanes, superchips for computers or drugs. The ability of individual nations or national firms to compete at the forefront of technology is rapidly declining. Advanced civil and military aircraft, for example, are made by international consortia (to name a few, Airbus, the Eurofighter and several helicopters). It is a step towards international co-operation but it is driven as much by commercial imperatives as any pan-European idealism. The trends in computers, where in America strategic alliances have formed between Apple and IBM or between Texas Instruments and others, are reflected in the alliance of Thomson-Bull in France and Motorola and NEC of Japan, or the takeover of ICL in the United Kingdom by Fujitsu. By recognising these trends the EU hopes to keep Europe ahead of the game or at least up with the front-runners. The Treaty specifies that the EU must take a long-term view. Also it is important to conduct common research projects so that, where new developments become commercially viable, they do so to a common EU standard, thus avoiding the product differentiation that has bedevilled the common market.

In 1994, the EU spent 3.6 per cent of its budget (ECU 2.8 billion) on research and technological development, and over the years there have been thousands of EU-supported transnational research projects; between 1983 and 1992 there were 2,576 laboratory link-ups and 3,884 joint research programmes. This exemplifies how widespread EU support is for science, and validates the EU's claim to be concerned with attaining technological parity with its main competitors. The Community has its own Joint Research Centre at nine institutes at Ispra (Italy), Karlsruhe (Germany), Petten (Netherlands) and Geel (Belgium). It is involved in research into such differing areas as nuclear fusion, AIDS and electronics.

The SEA also took note of other issues that did not dominate the thoughts of the founding fathers. By 1986, when the SEA was signed, environmental issues had come to the fore. A concern for the efficient use of resources had been expressed in the Treaty of Paris (ECSC), but the SEA went much further (Article 130r):

1. Action by the Community relating to the environment shall have the following objectives:
    (i) to preserve, protect and improve the quality of the environment;
    (ii) to contribute towards protecting human health;
    (iii) to ensure a prudent and rational utilisation of natural resources.

2. Action by the Community relating to the environment shall be based on the principles that preventive action should be taken, that environmental damage should as a priority be rectified at source, and that the polluter should pay. Environmental protection requirements shall be a

component of the Community's other policies.

3. In preparing its action relating to the environment the Community shall take account of:
  (i) available scientific and technical data;
  (ii) environmental conditions in the various regions of the Community;
  (iii) the potential benefits and costs of action or lack of action;
  (iv) the economic and social development of the Community as a whole and the balanced development of its regions.

It was agreed that EU action would be complementary to actions by Member States, and as in other parts of the Treaty such as environmental or social policy, where a Member State applied more stringent standards than the EU these would be left untouched.

The EU has been active in the environmental area, establishing common water-purity standards, or common car-exhaust limits, with catalysts being made mandatory in all new cars sold after January 1992, and pollution tests being added to annual mechanical tests (e.g. the MOT in the United Kingdom). In Clause 2 above it established two important principles, that preventive action should be taken and that the polluter should pay. This has led to much cat-calling, with Germany and France regarding Britain as the 'dirty man of Europe' and Britain casting around for counter-accusations. We are at the point now where the fight against pollution has become sufficiently serious for it to be seen as a money-making opportunity and this may change the rather insouciant attitude of the United Kingdom, with its relatively light-handed business regulation. The EU also recognises in Clause 3 that some states with a greater proportion of older industrial stock will have difficulties in meeting common standards, but that does not diminish the moral responsibility of the richer nations to clean up their own backyards. Importantly, Clause 2 also mentions that the EU will consider the environment when making decisions in other areas – so though the proportion of the Treaty devoted to the environment is small, its impact is pervasive.

CHAPTER 4

The Institutions

To read the papers or watch television, one would think that the Commission is the only significant institution within the EU. Occasionally the Council of Ministers is mentioned, and more often, now, the European Parliament, but their different roles are not really understood. The impression is that the Commission makes decisions and passes legislation that affects our daily lives: this is not the whole story. It is the Council which decides the programme for the EU and the Commission's job is to frame the relevant provisions – to put legislative meat on the bones of the Council's decisions – and then to present this to the European Parliament which may pass or amend and pass or reject the Council's proposals. (And, since Maastricht, the European Parliament may also put forward proposals.) Where the Commission does intervene in national affairs or the affairs of particular industries, for example, is *where EU law already exists*, whether it be preventing an anti-competitive merger or insisting on EU standards – as for water, drinking and on beaches – or fining countries that obstruct the free passage of goods, as when French farmers burn British sheep, break up Italian wine shipments or block Spanish tomatoes until they rot. However, the French are not the only culprits; the Commission had to intervene when the Germans blocked Cassis de Dijon, an alcoholic blackcurrant syrup added to wine, as it did not meet German liquor specifications which required a minimum alcohol content of 32 per cent in liqueurs, or when they tried to block British beer because it does not comply with the *Reinheitsgebot*, the national beer purity law. Other Member States have also been guilty of infringing EU law. The Commission is defined as the 'guardian' of EU law, a watchdog.

The institutions of the EU are the Council, the Commission, the European Parliament, the Court of Justice and the Court of Auditors. Apart from the last, they have all existed under all the treaties, *ab initio*, sometimes under different names. The Court of Auditors formally became institutionalised under revisions to the Treaty of Rome in 1977.

The directive body which decides the policy of the EU is the Council, which is composed of the relevant ministers from all the states; thus when the Council discusses financial policy, it is composed of the finance or economics ministers from each state (Ecofin); when it discusses agriculture it is composed of the agricultural ministers and so on. For some issues it acts by a qualified majority, but for most it acts by a simple majority. This was one of the changes enacted by the Maastricht Treaty. As the EU had grown, from 6 to 10, from 10 to 12 and then from 12 to 15 states, the previous principle of unanimity in the Council had become more and more unworkable, as single states – particularly the United Kingdom and the southern European states, whose perceived interests often differ from the majority's – voted against and blocked policies. To overcome the difficulties caused by this trend, Germany in particular has stated its desire to minimise the requirements for unanimity, wishing to invoke it only under the foreign-policy pillar of Maastricht where military decisions are involved (see Chapter 6, 'Foreign and security policy', pp. 127–130).

THE COUNCIL

The role of the Council is simply stated in Article 26 of the Treaty of Paris and Article 145 of the Treaty of Rome: it acts as a representative law-making forum for the governments of the Member States, and instructs the Commission as to policies that are to be carried out. Once policy has been decided, the Council informs the Commission as to its decisions, whereupon it is the Commission's role to prepare a proposal based on those decisions. The Council as finance ministers or ministers for agriculture meets once a month, while the other ministers meet twice a year.

Its remit is to co-ordinate the general economic policies of the Member States. It has the power to take decisions, and to delegate responsibility for their implementation to the Commission; it can also implement decisions directly itself. The procedures for doing so are to be agreed unanimously by the Council, on a proposal from the Commission, and require the opinion (though not the vote) of the European Parliament – a measure that edges towards reducing the democratic deficit.

The Council has one delegate from each Member State government, and originally the Presidency was held for six months in alternating six-year cycles as follows:

Cycle 1: Belgium, Denmark, Germany, Greece, Spain, France, Ireland, Italy, Luxembourg, Netherlands, Portugal, United Kingdom.
Cycle 2: Denmark, Belgium, Greece, Germany, France, Spain, Italy, Ireland, Netherlands, Luxembourg, United Kingdom, Portugal.

Cycle 1 was in alphabetic order (by national language – i.e. Germany is Deutschland, Greece is Ellas and Spain is Espana) and Cycle 2 simply swaps each pair around. At the time of writing (July 1995), Spain is in the chair with Italy to follow; that is, we are in the second cycle. Because of the accession of Austria, Sweden and Finland, a new arrangement will need to be formalised. It has been agreed to hold the Presidency in the following order until 2001:

	1st half	2nd half
1996	Italy	Ireland
1997	Netherlands	Luxembourg
1998	United Kingdom	Austria
1999	Germany	Finland
2000	Portugal	France
2001	Sweden	Belgium

The qualified majority

The qualified majority has caused a great deal of confusion among commentators, but if one breaks down the rules it is quite clear. Each Member State's delegate has a number of votes, based roughly on population size for the larger countries, but giving the smaller states an increased vote. The system was developed after the 'empty chair' crisis of 1965 when de Gaulle withdrew French representatives from the Council and later encouraged Gaullist MEPs to abstain from voting in the European Parliament. The other states had been happy to move to majority voting in the Council, but de Gaulle essentially wanted to maintain a veto. Qualified majority voting was the outcome, agreed in the so-called 'Luxembourg Compromise' of 1966.

There are three types of votes: unanimity, a simple majority and the qualified majority, which is required to agree the EU budget. Unanimity is self-defining: the only provision is that abstention does not prevent a unanimous agreement. The simple majority is a straight head count of the Member States' representatives. Originally, in the Treaty of Paris (which set up the ECSC), as modified by the Treaty of Rome, it specified that where there was an absolute majority at least two states with one-ninth of the EU's coal and steel production by value must be included, essentially so that small states could not railroad the larger states into agreeing on acts that went against their coal and steel interests. Where there is a deadlock, an act was deemed to have a majority if one side has three Member States with one-ninth of the EU's coal and steel by value. The pool of Member States from which such majorities can be drawn must therefore include in the former case two and, in the latter, three of the following countries: Germany, France, Italy and the United Kingdom.

The qualified majority weights the national representatives by size of country, as follows:

Belgium	5
Denmark	3
Germany	10
Greece	5

Spain	8
France	10
Ireland	3
Italy	10
Luxembourg	2
Netherlands	5
Austria	4
Portugal	5
Finland	3
Sweden	4
United Kingdom	10

There are thus a total of 87 votes; a qualified majority must be 62 *in favour* of a proposal (i.e. abstentions are not in favour, and are effectively votes against), with votes from not fewer than ten Member States. Thus if two large countries, say the United Kingdom and Italy, disagree with a budget proposal, then they need only two other countries in support (apart from Luxembourg) for the proposal to fail. If one large country disagrees, then it requires a total of 16 votes from the smaller countries to reject a measure. Conversely, if five small countries disagree with a measure, even if they do not have enough votes to stop it – e.g. Belgium, Denmark, Ireland, Luxembourg and Portugal, which give 18 votes – the measure will still be rejected because there are not more than eight states in favour. Thus the large states do generally have a high chance of having their way, but the small states are protected.

There are also rules governing relations with the other institutions. When 'co-operating' (under Article 189c, see Chapter 6) with the European Parliament on a proposal from the Commission, the Council has to adopt a 'common position', by qualified majority. It is then responsible for informing the European Parliament as to the reasons for its common position, and the Commission is also responsible for informing the Parliament as to its position. If Parliament agrees or fails to respond within three months, the 'Council shall definitively adopt the act in question in accordance with the common position'. Parliament can reject or amend by absolute majority; rejection effectively kills off an initiative unless the Council can unanimously agree to a second reading.

Where a common position is amended, the Commission must within one month forward the Parliament's amendments to the Council, together with comments on amendments with which it does not agree. It requires a qualified majority in the Council to accept the amendments the Commission has agreed, and unanimity to amend an altered proposal which the Commission has accepted. If the Council does nothing about a proposal for three months then it is dropped, though with the agreement of the European Parliament this period can be extended by one further month. The Commission can also alter any proposal while it is with the Council, if the Council has not yet acted.

The Council's further responsibility is to decide the salaries of the Commission and of the Court of Justice.

The Council is assisted by the Committee of Permanent Representatives (COREPER – its French acronym), whose members are civil servants, appointees of the Member States. COREPER was set up in 1965 to assist the Council; it does the groundwork for Council meetings and handles Council business between meetings. It assesses Commission proposals, often because the Council has inadequate time to discuss them, and it is also the route through which the Commission initially contacts Member State governments before drawing up proposals. Permanent Representatives deputise for ministers unable to attend Council meetings; they hold ambassadorial rank. Because of COREPER's professional, full-time intermediary role it effectively often makes decisions which the Council itself simply rubber-stamps, which has been seen as contributing to the 'democratic deficit' (see elsewhere).

Alan Clark (UK Minister of Trade in 1986) commented on COREPER's influence in his *Diaries*:

... Not, really, that it makes the slightest difference to the conclusions of a meeting what Ministers say at it. Everything is decided, horse-traded off, by officials at COREPER ... The Ministers arrive on the scene at the last minute, hot, tired, ill, or drunk (sometimes all of these together), read out their piece and depart.

Clark thought this was odd as the constitution of the EC was quite clear and the Council of Ministers has complete authority over COREPER. However, officials have a grasp of the minutiae that ministers do not have time for and can, effectively, present them with *faits accomplis* when the latter turn up for signing sessions.

European Council

There is also the '*European* Council' which consists of the heads of state and government and which meets at least twice a year. Quite distinct from the Council of Ministers, effectively this is a summit meeting and is often referred to as such. The role of the European Council is to set the political agenda for the EU, in essence to sustain the political momentum. Sometimes its work is slowed down by the need to find solutions to problems that the other institutions of the EU cannot resolve. Decisions reached at the European Council have to go through the usual legislative procedures before they can become EU law.

THE COMMISSION

The Commission has 20 members, two from the larger countries, one from the smaller. The UK convention is to propose one from the Labour Party and one from the Conservatives (currently Neil Kinnock and Sir Leon Brittan respectively). No Member State has less than one member – none has more than two. There is a President of the Commission; currently (1995) Jacques Santer of Luxembourg holds the office. His predecessor was Jacques Delors, who became a bogeyman to some sections of the British political establishment – particularly the Eurosceptic right of the Conservative Party – and something of a hero to others, namely some trades unions and the Labour Party. Delors greatly raised the profile of the office, so much so perhaps that many people lost sight of the fact that the Commission is an executive organisation; that is, it does not decide what the aims of legislation will be – that is for the European Council, with the approval of the European Parliament. The Commission's role is to ensure that the Council's decisions are converted into proposals, which define the Council's aims in detailed legal form. That said, the Commission does have a great deal of influence in that it frames all the proposals that are the basis of EU law. It has the exclusive right – though this may change given the European Parliament's desire for more executive power and hints of moves in this direction given by the Treaty of Maastricht – the so-called 'right of initiative', to withdraw or modify a proposal at any time during the legislative process. To assist the President in his duties there are one or two Vice-Presidents; originally there were six in the Treaty of Rome, but this was amended by Maastricht. The period of office for Presidents and Vice-Presidents is two years, renewable.

Commissioners hold office for five-year renewable terms (originally four, but increased so as to match the term of the European Parliament); they exercise responsibility over specific aspects of the Commission's activities. For example, Karel Van Miert is currently responsible for competition, ensuring that EU rules are observed in Member States. (Commissioners and their briefs are listed in Appendix 2.)

All Commissioners are supposed to be totally independent of their nation state. Article 10 of the Merger Treaty declares:

> The members of the Commission shall, in the general interest of the Communities, be completely independent in the performance of their duties.
>
> In the performance of these duties, they shall neither seek nor take instruction from any Government or from any other body. They shall refrain from any action incompatible with their duties. Each Member State undertakes to respect this principle and not to seek to influence the members of the Commission in the performance of their tasks.

While they are Commissioners they are not allowed to engage in any other activity, whether gainful or not. The legislation constructing the Commission was framed, insofar as is possible, to ensure that the Commission became a supranational body, which would come to perceive and to hold to the interests of the Union as a whole. In many respects it has done so, as is shown by the anguished cries within the relevant states when 'their' Commissioner rules against them on an issue. (Sir Leon Brittan fining chemical companies, including ICI for acting in a cartel with several other European companies, is a recent example.) There is also the phenomenon of new Commissioners, among other EU officials, going 'native' or 'living in a Brussels ivory tower' – varied ways of saying that they have adopted a different viewpoint from the narrow national interest after living in the most concentratedly 'European' environment. The Treaty was firm in stating that Member States had to respect the independence of their national Commissioners, without mandating them to follow government instructions. In general this has been adhered to, but even Jacques Delors put national interests in front of the EU's when he caused the postponement of Commission condemnation of illegal subsidies to a French textile firm. Where a Commissioner is deemed to have failed in his responsibilities, or misbehaved, the Council or Commission can apply to the Court of Justice to have him compulsorily retired. To date this power has not been exercised.

From the description of the role of the Council, it might appear that the Commission is relatively powerless and simply responds to Council decisions. But the Council can only debate proposals as formulated by the Commission. In other words, the Council can nominate the destination but it is the Commission that decides the route. In theory, the Commission decides how to act by a simple majority, which given that there are 20 members could make decision-making difficult, but in practice it operates by consensus. The only exception to this is when, for whatever reason, there is a vacancy. Here, the Council decides whether to replace the missing Commissioner.

The Commission issues its instructions in three ways:

1. *Regulations*, which apply throughout the EU, and which are binding 'and directly applicable in all Member States', that is they take the force of law, without need for further action by Member States. They take priority over national law where the two conflict. This principle was established in 1963 by the *van Gend en Loos* case and reaffirmed in the *Costa v. ENEL* case of 1964.

2. *Directives*, which are binding on Member States, but the Member State can choose the means of enforcement; that is, they enact national legislation to reflect the meaning of the directive.

Recently the Court of Appeal in the United Kingdom held that 1985 legislation barring workers who had worked less than two years from suing for unfair dismissal breached a 1972 directive against discrimination on sexual grounds, as the two-year rule affected women more than men. At the time of writing the Department of Trade and Industry was considering an appeal, since this ruling opened the way to a barrage of claims. Whatever the outcome of the appeal, this case shows the acceptance of the principle that where they conflict, EU law takes precedence over national law. In 1991 in the *Francovich* case it was also established that where a directive confers rights on an individual, a Member State (in this case Italy) could be held liable for damages if that directive were not properly implemented by that state; and recently (1995) in the United Kingdom, the government was required to compensate two women who had suffered sexual harassment on a Tunisian package tour, because a 1990 package-tour directive made tour operators liable for the negligence of suppliers (in this case the Tunisian hotel operators who did not instruct staff how to behave properly towards the two women). In other words, as a means of enforcement, governments are held liable; if the directives had been implemented properly by the Italian and the British governments, it would have been Francovich's employer who compensated him, and the two women would have been compensated by the tour operator.

3. *Decisions*, which are binding in their entirety, but apply to specific named parties.

There are also two levels of non-compulsory advice, *Recommendations* and *Opinions*. They could be described as hints of decreasing severity, which are usually taken into account by their recipients. Regulations are published in the *Official Journal of the Community* and take effect either on the date specified or twenty days after publication. Decisions take effect when the recipient is notified, and where they impose fines or other costs on their recipients, such obligations are enforceable through the national courts of the relevant Member State. The *Official Journal* appears on a daily basis, with Regulations being published roughly a week after they are signed by a Commissioner. An issue often contains two or three items per day and is published in three series, the 'L' series containing legislation. This gives some idea of the extraordinary volume of legal activity in which the Commission is engaged.

In the interests of open government – there is much concern in the EU over the so-called democratic deficit – the Council and Commission have to publish the reasons underlying any decision they make. In addition, the Commission is responsible for publishing an annual report on the activities of the Communities.

The Commission is also responsible for relations with the UN and the GATT, and is given an open brief with regard to other international organisations (Article 229). For example, Sir Leon Brittan was much involved in the final brinksmanship of the Uruguay Round, where the EU and the United States only resolved their differences over agricultural subsidies at the last minute.

Functioning of the Commission

As mentioned above, the Commission decides on issues by majority voting. This only applies to what might be described as major decisions, however. For minor decisions there is the 'written procedure', whereby proposals are circulated to Commissioners and are adopted automatically where no objection is raised. The Commissioners are in charge of directorates (see list in Appendix 2) which are run by directors, usually of a different nationality from their own. Commissioners are supported by a *chef de cabinet*, a small personal office, and the staff of the directorates they supervise.

The total staff of the Commission runs to about 15,000 employees, of whom approximately one in eight are interpreters and translators. This is about as many bureaucrats as are employed by a London borough – none of whom, one hopes, need to be interpreters – and gives the lie to the idea of a swollen bureaucracy at the apex of the EU. The cost of EU bureaucracy was

ECU 2.9 billion in 1992, which was 4.66 per cent of the total budget. It also explains why the Commission can be slow in dealing with issues, given that it has to deal with so many differing national legislatures and procedures for adopting EU law.

The Economic and Social Committee

The Commission is assisted by a consultative committee, the Economic and Social Committee. Article 193 describes its composition:

> The Committee shall consist of representatives of the various categories of economic and social activity, in particular, representatives of producers, farmers, carriers, workers, dealers, craftsmen, professional occupation and representatives of the general public.

This definition basically allows for three blocs – employers, unions and what are described as 'various interests', essentially independent representatives put forward by political parties in the Member States. It has 222 members drawn from the various states as follows:

Belgium	12
Denmark	9
Germany	24
Greece	12
Spain	21
France	24
Ireland	9
Italy	24
Luxembourg	6
Netherlands	12
Austria	12
Portugal	12
Finland	9
Sweden	12
United Kingdom	24

Its members are appointed for four-year terms by the Council, in consultation with the Commission, from candidates nominated by Member States who put forward two candidates for each position. To reflect the merger of the various institutions of the Communities, Article 197 makes special provision for two of the other titles of the Treaty: 'In particular, it shall contain an agricultural section and a transport section, which are the subject of special provisions in the Titles relating to agriculture and transport.'

It is also laid down that members are to be representatives, not delegates; that is, they are not supposed to act under external mandates. The role of this Committee is to assist the Commission; the Commission outlines its objectives and programmes and the Consultative Committee responds with its recommendations as to the provisions that should be included. As the Commission does not have to abide by its recommendations, though, there are doubts as to its value and one commentator even described it as looking 'like a bloated freebie!' There have been suggestions for its abolition – 222 members make it a rather unwieldy body and it has no means of enforcing its conclusions on the Commission – but the Maastricht Treaty in effect reinforced its existence by creating the parallel Committee of the Regions, which shares the same facilities and secretariat. Also, despite publicity shots showing it in full (packed) session, a large proportion of its members find it difficult to attend regularly due to other commitments, and in practice it is less unwieldy than the head count suggests.

THE EUROPEAN PARLIAMENT

The role of the European Parliament has expanded over the years. Initially, it was little more than a rubber stamp for the Commission, but gradually it has acquired more power and now exercises 'advisory and supervisory powers'. This is partly in response to the enlargement of the European Community over the years – with the arrival of countries like Denmark or Sweden which prefer a more open and accountable system of government than countries like the United Kingdom and France – and partly to reduce the 'democratic deficit' that results from the directive power of the Council, whose decision-making process is closed to outside observers. Until the 1979 election, Members of the European

Parliament were nominated by the national Parliaments, thus in a sense exacerbating the democratic deficit as the composition of national groups of MEPs would reflect the existing order within their Member States. Members are now directly elected.

The Parliament is composed of 626 MPs in proportion (roughly) to the population of the countries, with an exception being made for Luxembourg. When Germany was reunited, it requested an extra 18 seats in the European Parliament and this request was granted. The Parliament has also grown with the accession of new members. Its current composition (previous composition in brackets) is as follows:

Belgium	25	(24)
Denmark	16	(16)
Germany	99	(81)
Greece	25	(24)
Spain	64	(60)
France	87	(81)
Ireland	15	(15)
Italy	87	(81)
Luxembourg	6	(6)
Netherlands	31	(25)
Austria	21	
Portugal	25	(24)
Finland	16	
Sweden	22	
United Kingdom	87	(81)

Elections are held by direct universal suffrage in all Member States, though Member States employ differing electoral systems that reflect their national electoral traditions – differing types of proportional representation apply in all Member States apart from Ireland and Northern Ireland (single transferable votes) and the United Kingdom which clings to the 'first past the post' method. Ultimately the intention is that voting should be carried out by a uniform electoral procedure, though no deadline has been fixed. Voting throughout the EU has to take place between the same Thursday and Sunday, so as to ensure it is as free – not influenced by the outcome in other states – as possible. Members are elected to serve for five years. The European Parliament annual session begins on the second Tuesday in March, though it can be convened by the Council, the Commission or at the request of a majority of its members. In an election year, it meets for its first plenary session on the first Tuesday that falls after a month has elapsed since the election closed. The European Parliament also elects its own President and officers, and draws up its own rules of procedure. It makes decisions by an absolute majority.

The rights of MEPs were clearly set out in the 1976 'Act concerning the election of the representatives of the European Parliament by direct universal suffrage':

1. Representatives shall vote on an individual and personal basis. They shall not be bound by any instructions and shall not receive a binding mandate.

2. Representatives shall enjoy the privileges and immunities applicable to members of the European Parliament by virtue of the Protocol on the Privileges and Immunities of the European Communities annexed to the Treaty establishing a Single Council and a Single Commission of the European Communities.

It is permissible for an MP, a member of a national legislature, to be an MEP, but not a member of government in a Member State, apart from in the United Kingdom where it is considered impossible from a practical viewpoint for a person to serve in both. It is not permissible for MEPs to be employed in any capacity in any other EU organisation.

The President of the Commission has the right to attend sessions of the European Parliament, and can request speaking time. In turn the Commission has to respond to questions presented by the European Parliament. Members of the Council have similar rights to the President of the Commission in regard to the European Parliament. The European Parliament also debates the Commission's annual report (see above) and has the right to censure it and, if necessary, with a two-thirds majority it can force the Commission to resign. In October 1995 it threatened to do this if the Commission did not more actively pursue France for the Mururoa atomic tests under the safety provisions of the EAEC treaty; the EC sent observers to whom the French rather grudgingly released information – the Mururoa tests and the protests they evoke are still alive at the time of writing. It also has the right to approve a new Commission, and the current Commission was the first which had to receive Parliamentary approval. It has some control over the budget, as it can reject draft budgets in their entirety, also the power to amend the budget in that it can transfer expenditure from one area to another, i.e. it does not increase total spending, and the Council has to vote to *reject* such amendments and has 15 days to do so. Where the European Parliament proposes increased expenditure, the Council has to *approve* these, otherwise such proposals lapse. In general, its powers have been greatly enhanced by the 'co-operation' procedure (see pp. 124–127).

The European Parliament meets in Strasbourg and Luxembourg, with most committee meetings taking place in Brussels. This is seen by many as an absurd waste of resources: the time spent by MEPs in making their way from one location to the next, the duplication of facilities, the vast trains of interpreters and other support staff wending their way across Northern Europe. It is as if the British Parliament held sessions in London and Coventry, with support staff based in Coventry and committee meetings taking place in York!

There is a further problem with the European Parliament for the smaller countries. Philosophically, the idea of the Parliament being granted greater powers leads to more democratic accountability, and is thus a 'good thing' but – because the number of seats a country holds is in proportion to its population – where issues are dominated by national rather than party political considerations, clearly they are in a minority, whereas in the Council – because of the requirements for unanimity or the qualified majority – they have much more influence. Minority rights are always a difficult issue, and the European Parliament proves no exception.

The powers of the European Parliament have been extended by

the Maastricht Treaty (see Chapter 6) and their further extension will be one of the main issues facing the 1996 Intergovernmental Conference. In the meantime, under the Presidency of Klaus Haensch, some apparently minor but important procedural changes have been made:

1. Until recently voting was carried out on Wednesday evenings, which meant both that any decision could not be published in the newspapers till Friday morning, when the result would be less newsworthy, and that some MEPs would find it difficult to attend and therefore vote – hardly democratic. Voting is now carried out on Tuesday and Wednesday at midday, which increases the opportunities for MEPs to vote and for the newspapers to carry outcomes the following day.

2. Plenary sessions now have intervals so that the relevant parliamentary committees can meet to discuss the progress of debates.

3. Question Time (a procedure adopted from the UK Parliament) now groups related topics, so as to speed up business and so that the MEPs with particular interests know at what times they should definitely attend.

4. Travel allowances for MEPs have been halved! – not in the same category as the above changes, but undoubtedly heartening to most readers. There were many reports of MEPs claiming the full fare for a journey, then booking a cheap ticket and pocketing the difference. This should now be more difficult.

THE COURT OF JUSTICE

The Court of Justice consists of 13 judges, assisted by six Advocates-General. They are appointed for six years, with six or seven of the judges and three Advocates-General being replaced alternately every three years. The judges also appoint a President of the Court every three years from among their number. All terms are renewable.

The role of the Court of Justice is to be the ultimate arbiter in the EU where there is any dispute as to the interpretation of EU rules: 'The Court of Justice shall ensure that in the interpretation and application of this Treaty the law is observed' (Article 164). It can declare the regulations or decisions of the Commission or Council void in specific instances; these are where the Commission has:

(a) shown a lack of competence;
(b) committed an infringement of essential procedure;
(c) infringed the Treaty or the laws relating to its application; or
(d) committed an abuse of powers.

Member States applying for redress on these grounds must bring the action within two months of being aware of a particular measure. Individuals and companies (legal persons, i.e. corporations) may also start proceedings against the Commission or Council if they are directly affected. In September 1995, for example, the Court of Justice ruled against the Commission after the latter had dismissed a complaint by Ladbroke's (a British leisure/gambling company) that it had been excluded from the French market by Pari Mutuel Urbain, a clear breach of competition rules.

In cases where, contrary to the provisions of the Treaty, the Council or Commission fails to act, then a party can give two months' notice, and if these institutions still fail to respond they can be taken to the Court within two months. The Commission has duties under the Treaty to make decisions and recommendations, and where it does not do so the Member States can ask it to do so under (d) above.

The Commission also applies to the Court where a Member State fails to fulfil its obligations under the Treaty. The Commission delivers an opinion after that Member State has given an explanation of its actions, and if the Member State does not comply within the period laid down in that opinion, then the Commission may apply to the Court of Justice. Member States can also apply to the Court if they feel another Member State has acted wrongly, though only after bringing the matter before the Commission, which has three months to deliver an opinion which may or may not be acted on. If the Commission does not respond within three months, the case may still be brought before the Court. Member States are bound by the judgement of the Court.

The Court can only enforce any fines it has imposed after the recipient has had time to comment on them. If the recipient appeals, the Court has unlimited jurisdiction in any appeal against any fine.

As well as having to submit to the Court in the circumstances outlined above, the Commission can also apply to the Court to declare acts of the European Parliament or the Council void. For the European Parliament, the Commission must apply to the Court within one month of publication or notification of an act of the European Parliament, and is limited in such applications to cases where the European Parliament has shown a lack of competence or infringed a procedure. Member States have the same rights as the Commission in this respect.

The Court can issue interim injunctions, though the mere bringing of a case intended to stop some activity does not mean that the activity will be automatically suspended. As well as injunctions, the Court can impose any orders it sees fit. It can also order the EU to pay compensation where an employee of the EU has done wrong in the course of his or her duties, though any other disputes between the EU and other parties come under the jurisdiction of national courts. The Court also has jurisdiction over contracts signed by the EU where an arbitration clause in the contract so provides, and over provisions of the Treaty where Member States' legislation confers it. The Member States have agreed that the Court's judgements are enforceable in their territory (Article 44), via local legal machinery.

The Court also acts in other matters, as under Article 177:

The Court of Justice shall have jurisdiction to give preliminary rulings concerning:
(a) the interpretation of this Treaty;
(b) the validity and interpretation of acts of the institutions of the Community;

(c) the interpretation of the statutes of bodies established by an act of the Council, where those statutes so provide.

Courts or tribunals within Member States can apply for rulings on EU law, and when judicial remedies on such matters are beyond the competence of national courts these courts are expected to refer the matter to the Court of Justice. If there is no further appeal under a national legal system where such a ruling is necessary, then the national courts must seek a ruling. The Court also arbitrates in internal disputes within EU institutions relating to staff regulations and conditions of employment. The European Investment Bank is also ultimately answerable to the Court, but only where Member States or the Commission complain. Finally, the Court is often specified as the arbiter in contracts made by the Community.

So far the Court has played an active role, interpreting EU provisions in a way that furthers the impetus of European union; it is thus dynamic rather than reactive and has no fear of asserting its independence. It found that the Greek government had acted illegally in providing ECU 170 million of government aid to Heracles, the state-owned cement manufacturer, in a case brought by Italian, British and private Greek manufacturers, and that the subsidy should be withdrawn. With the PVC cartel, it first of all declared that a Commission fine had been illegal because documents had not been properly translated for the benefit of participants (which included in Germany: BASF, Wacker Chemie, Huls; in the United Kingdom: ICI and Shell International Chemical; in the Netherlands: DSM; in Belgium: Limburgse Vinyl Maatshappij; in Italy: Enichem and Montedison; in France: Elf Atochem and Société de Vinyl de France) which was a proper application of natural justice; then when the Commission re-submitted its case, properly translated, the Court accepted the case and fined the cartel ECU 23.5 million. It is afraid to take on neither governments nor large and powerful companies. Its main problem has simply been the weight of cases brought before it – hence the formalisation of the Court of First Instance. It has also come under attack, most recently by a German judge, from those who dispute the superiority of EU law over national law, despite the general acceptance of this principle.

The Court of First Instance was established initially to relieve the Court of Justice, and its judgements were only appealable to the Court of Justice on points of law, i.e. interpretation. Its role has expanded beyond hearing cases against the Commission; it can now act on cases brought to annul EU legislation or failure to observe it. Neither court should be confused with the Court of Human Rights in Strasbourg, which was set up under the Convention for the Protection of Human Rights. This was signed under the auspices of the Council of Europe – not an EU organisation, as the EU has not yet signed up to the Convention – in Rome in 1950. This 'European' court was the court that found against the United Kingdom in the Gibraltar IRA killings.

THE COURT OF AUDITORS

Understandably, given that Member States agreed to contribute percentages of their tax revenues to the budget of the EU, as well as sometimes paying to join the EU as the United Kingdom did, they wanted to be sure that their money was being spent effectively and legally, and to check the accounts of the EU as presented by the Commission in its annual account. Hence the formation of the Court of Auditors in 1977. It has to be said that the Court is not renowned for its rigour in cutting down fraud, which has had various estimates put on it – up to 10 per cent of EU funds, according to one source. But recently Member States have agreed that it needs to be more stringent. It already has sweeping powers of investigation where the institutions of the EU are concerned and with their national counterparts in Member States. What has been lacking perhaps is a sense of accountability at the centre and a reluctance to disturb the feathers of Member States which do not effectively police internal fraud. But as EU budgets have escalated, and the increase in the rate of growth has slowed, some Member States have protested and insisted that task forces be set up to root out known and suspected areas of fraud.

The Court of Auditors draws up an annual report on EU expenditure at the end of each financial year, which is published

in the *Official Journal of the European Communities* after comment by
the various Community institutions. The Court was institutionalised under Maastricht; whereas previously it had no powers to
enforce its views, it can now do so in the Court of Justice.

THE EUROPEAN INVESTMENT BANK (EIB)

The task of the European Investment Bank shall be to
contribute, by having recourse to the capital market and
utilising its own resources, to the balanced and steady
development of the common market in the interest of the
Community. For this purpose the Bank shall, operating on a
non-profit-making basis, grant loans and give guarantees
which facilitate the financing of the following projects in all
sectors of the economy:

(a) projects for developing less-developed regions;
(b) projects for modernising or converting undertakings
or for developing fresh activities called for by the progressive establishment of the common market, where
these projects are of such a size or nature that they
cannot be entirely financed by the various means available in the individual Member States;
(c) projects of common interest to several Member States
which are of such a size or nature that they cannot be
entirely financed by the various means available in the
individual Member States.

So begins the Treaty, clearly setting out its intention to create a
version of the World Bank for Europe, essentially by setting up an
institution that can offer soft loans to the poorer members of the
EU by transferring capital from the richer.

The provisions governing the activities in which the EIB may
engage are described in the general provisions of the Treaty of
Rome in the Protocol on the Statute of the European Investment
Bank. All Member States are members of the Bank, though they
subscribed different proportions of the capital:

Germany, France, Italy, United Kingdom	20 per cent each
Spain	7 per cent
Belgium, the Netherlands	5.3 per cent each
All other states together	7.7 per cent

The initial capital subscription was ECU 28,800 million, the ECU being described as the 'unit of account' (EUA) used by the European Communities. The Board of Governors consists of Ministers designated by Member States. The Bank has 22 directors, three each from the leading subscribers, two from Spain, and one from each of the remaining Member States.

Article 20 of the protocol lists the principles under which the Bank should operate:

1. It shall ensure that its funds are employed as rationally as possible in the interests of the Community.
    It may grant loans or guarantees only:
    (a) where, in the case of projects carried out by undertakings in the production sector, interest and amortisation payments are covered out of operating profits or, in other cases, either by a commitment entered into by the State in which the project is carried out or by some other means; and
    (b) where the execution of the project contributes to an increase in economic productivity in general and promotes the attainment of the common market.

2. It shall neither acquire any interest in an undertaking nor assume any responsibility in its management unless this is required to safeguard the rights of the Bank in ensuring recovery of funds lent.

3. It may dispose of its claims on the capital market and may, to this end, require its debtors to issue bonds or other securities.

It is made clear from the outset that the Bank is not supposed to offer grants disguised as loans, nor is its job to speculate or become involved in day-to-day management. Undertakings can apply for loans either through the Commission or through their own Member State or direct to the Bank. Both the Commission and the Member State must be consulted for an opinion; if they do not deliver this within two months, then the Bank can assume that there is no objection to the proposed loan.

Annually, the EIB makes loans of around 20 billion ECU, mostly within the EU but also around the world – helping the economies of Eastern Europe and Mediterranean non-member countries, participating in the Middle East peace process with loans to Lebanon and Gaza, aiding the 70 signatories of the Lomé Convention, and Latin America and Asia. After the Essen European Council of December 1994, it set up special facilities to assist in the priority projects that the Council identified. It has therefore paid particular attention to funding the TENs and to other long-term projects that will assist European recovery.

The EIB is not to be confused with the European Bank for Reconstruction and Development which began operations in 1991, with the purpose of aiding the restructuring and development of the economies of Central and Eastern Europe and the former Soviet Union. The aim, while in itself entirely commendable, was not entirely matched by the early history of the EBRD. As with so many EU institutions there was a row as to where to locate the Bank's headquarters, with London and Frankfurt emerging as the main contenders. London – after some horse-trading, namely agreeing that the Bank's president would be French – won, but this victory was followed by scandal. The building that the Bank was to occupy had recently been completed. The person chosen to head the Bank, Jacques Attali – brother of the then French finance minister Bernard Attali – proceeded to have the interior ripped out and replaced at a cost of £750,000. Private aircraft were hired at a cost of £600,000, and in its first two years the Bank spent £200 million on itself – twice the amount it invested in Eastern Europe. This hardly accorded with its aims. Before even opening it had spent millions of pounds of European taxpayers' money, money which would have been very helpful if used for the purpose for which it was intended. Scandal continued to dog the Bank, with evidence surfacing of ridiculous expenses being incurred. The Commission and the contributors to the Bank moved to redress the situation: Attali had to resign in June 1993, and the Bank was ordered to institute a less wasteful regime.

THE EUROPEAN ATOMIC ENERGY COMMUNITY (EAEC)

Nuclear energy was seen by many as the fuel of the future when the EEC was founded in 1957, and it had been decided that at the same time there should exist institutions which paralleled those of the ECSC for an orderly and open nuclear market. There is much less enthusiasm for nuclear power now, partly due to events like the Chernobyl explosion and the Three Mile Island accident in Pennsylvania, and partly due to the realisation of the immense difficulties and huge costs of decommissioning plant, with nobody really knowing how to safely store spent nuclear fuel, or the parts of nuclear plants which have become radioactively contaminated. The half-lives of these toxic materials extend for thousands, sometimes tens of thousands, of years. Dumping them at sea is no longer regarded as safe, at least for any length of time, and burial underground can affect ground-water systems. Decommissioning costs are now taken into account when planning for the commissioning of new plant, and rather than being what it was once perceived as – a source of abundant, virtually free energy – nuclear power is now seen as a potentially dangerous, almost certainly expensive route to energy independence. France remains the main enthusiast for nuclear power in Europe, because of its complete dependence on external sources of oil; it even exports nuclear-powered electricity to the United Kingdom.

The provisions of the Treaty setting up the EAEC are very similar to those of the ECSC, the aims being set out in the very first articles:

It shall be the task of the Community to contribute to the raising of the standard of living in the Member States and to the development of relations with the other countries by creating the conditions necessary for the speedy establishment and growth of nuclear industries.

In order to perform its task, the Community shall, as provided in this Treaty:

(a) promote research and ensure the dissemination of technical information;

(b) establish uniform safety standards to protect the health of workers and of the general public and ensure that they are applied;

(c) facilitate investment and ensure, particularly by encouraging ventures on the part of undertakings, the establishment of the basic installations necessary for the development of nuclear energy in the Community;

(d) ensure that all users in the Community receive a regular and equitable supply of ores and nuclear fuels;

(e) make certain, by appropriate supervision, that nuclear materials are not diverted to purposes other than those for which they are intended;

(f) exercise the right of ownership conferred upon it with respect to special fissile materials;

(g) ensure wide commercial outlets and access to the best technical facilities by the creation of a common market in specialised materials and equipment, by the free movement of capital for investment in the field of nuclear energy and by freedom of employment for specialists within the Community;

(h) establish with other countries and international organisations such relations as will foster progress in the peaceful uses of nuclear energy.

The institutions of the EAEC were the same as for the EEC and the ECSC, but were brought together in the Merger Treaty. The Commission was given a wide-ranging role in the promotion and directing of research. The fruits of any research programmes it had initiated were to be made available to all suitable undertakings; its inspectors were granted rights of access to all plants in the Community; an Agency was set up, under the control of the Commission, to source nuclear materials within and without the Community and to make them generally available to users. The Agency has right of first refusal on such supplies, and where it does not take advantage of this, suppliers of nuclear materials are allowed to sell their products on the international market subject to approval by the Commission.

PRIVILEGES OF THE COMMUNITY

The Community or Union is regarded as a sovereign state, its personnel being treated as diplomats with freedom to travel without restraint through EU countries. Where there is any legal dispute between the Union and a third party over its property or assets, action can only be taken against the Union with the authorisation of the Court of Justice. EU property is exempt from 'search, requisition, confiscation or expropriation', and thus has the same rights as accredited diplomatic missions throughout the EU. EU communications are treated as diplomatic and are not to be interfered with, interrupted or censored.

More controversially, EU personnel are not subject to national direct taxes, which has given rise to charges of Brussels feather-bedding. The direct taxes they pay are to the EU, and are not regarded as onerous. The EU even claims back its indirect taxes (i.e. VAT) on 'movable and immovable' property, though generously it agrees to pay such taxes on utilities, its water, electricity and telephone bills. EU staff do pay income tax to the EU itself; the rate varies from 10 to 45 per cent depending on marital status, family situation etc. They do not benefit from tax relief for cars and mortgages and they have to pay local (i.e. residential – the Council Tax in the United Kingdom, for example) taxes. EU employee salaries are published in the *Official Journal of the European Communities*.

MEPs are granted the same rights as MPs within their own countries, and it is specifically forbidden for Member States to penalise them in any way if in the course of their duties they vote or express opinions in ways that displease the government of their Member State. They are also accorded diplomatic rights for travel within the EU. Similarly, EU officials are granted legal immunity, in perpetuity, for anything they have done in an official capacity. Third-country nationals accredited to the Community – that is ambassadors and diplomatic missions – receive the same diplomatic immunities as if they were accredited to sovereign states.

CHAPTER 5

The Single European Act (SEA)

This Act, signed in 1986, was another step down the road to fuller integration. Although quite brief, it contains declarations that fly in the face of those who claim that the European Union is not more than a customs union, a free-trade zone. The preamble alone contains declarations that would incense the true Europhobe:

> Moved by the will to continue the work undertaken on the basis of the Treaties establishing the European Communities and to transform relations as a whole among their States in a European Union, in accordance with the Solemn Declaration of Stuttgart of 19 June 1983,

> Resolved to implement this European Union on the basis, firstly, of the Communities operating in accordance with their own rules and, secondly, of European Co-operation among the Signatory States in the *sphere of foreign policy and to invest this union with the necessary means of action.*

> Determined to work together to promote democracy on the basis of the fundamental rights recognised in the constitutions and laws of the Member States, in the Convention for the Protection of Human Rights and Fundamental Freedoms and the European Social Charter, notably *freedom, equality and social justice.*

Convinced that the *European idea*, the results achieved in the fields of economic integration and political co-operation, and the need for new developments correspond to the wishes of the democratic peoples of Europe, for whom the European Parliament, elected by universal suffrage, is an indispensable means of expression,

Aware of the *responsibility incumbent upon Europe to aim at speaking ever increasingly with one voice* and to act with consistency and solidarity in order more effectively to protect its common interests and independence, in particular to display the principles of democracy and compliance with the law and with human rights to which they are attached, so that together they may make their own contribution to the preservation of international peace and security in accordance with the undertaking entered into by them within the framework of the United Nations Charter,

Determined to improve the economic and social situation by *extending common policies* and pursuing new objectives, and to ensure a smoother functioning of the Communities by enabling the institutions to exercise powers under conditions most in keeping with Community interests ... [author's italics throughout]

The whole sense of a sea-change in attitudes is contained in this preamble. It is the 'European idea' which now infuses the actions of the Member States. The idea has now become part of the basic way they think, European institutions no longer being an experiment or an artificial entity. The SEA declared effectively that in all external matters, Member States would expect to act primarily through the EU, and that in internal matters involving common issues, such as social justice, Member States would be guided by the decisions of the EU. The first Article of the Act states that the European Communities and European Political Co-operation shall aim to make 'concrete progress towards European unity'.

'European Political Co-operation' is a declaration by the Member States that they intend to forge common positions on matters of foreign policy: foreign ministers meet at least four times a year under its aegis to develop common positions for joint action. Member States are expected to consult each other before taking any action, and to attempt to take account of the positions of other Member States on any given issue. In this they are to closely involve the Commission and the European Parliament. The aim was to develop programmes based on common principles and objectives, and these programmes would then guide the policies of the Member States.

Where matters are put to the vote, it was agreed at Maastricht (Declaration 27) that where a qualified majority existed, Member States were not to jeopardise unanimity. The minority – once it discovers it is the minority – is expected to renounce its contrary vote and toe the line, though how this can be effected in practice is a different issue.

Provisions are made for co-operation in security and in 'technological and industrial conditions necessary for their security', namely jointly sustaining a European defence industry. As part of this, greater co-operation with the Western European Union (WEU) and NATO was to be put in hand. There is much co-operation in this field, with the development of the European fighter aircraft to replace the Tornado – itself a European co-operation – being jointly undertaken by France, Germany, Spain and the United Kingdom, and a well-established tradition of co-operation in helicopters – though recently the United Kingdom opted for the US-made Apache rather than developing a Euro-copter with France and Germany, as did the Netherlands. Missile systems are also jointly made, though (because of the size of national defence industries) in France, the United Kingdom and Germany, for historical reasons, separate national systems have also been developed. Nor is there any common armoured vehicle programme, though Germany has sold tanks and associated vehicles to a number of European countries. Development programmes for new weapons have become increasingly expensive over the last few years (the European fighter's development alone will cost at least $20 billion). Part of the WEU's remit is to work towards creating a European armaments agency.

The SEA also changed Council vote requirements from unanimity to a qualified majority in many areas of policy-making. It also set down the deadline for the achievement of a single European market:

> The Community shall adopt measures with the aim of progressively establishing the internal market over a period expiring on 31 December 1992 ... The internal market shall comprise an area without internal frontiers in which the free movement of goods, persons, services and capital is ensured in accordance with the provisions of this Treaty.

Lord Cockfield, the United Kingdom's Commissioner at the time, was charged with the duty of setting out the proposals to make this a reality. He came up with 282 proposals, of which 264 were enacted by the deadline (see the Cecchini Report, pp. 93–102)

The SEA also declared its intention of beefing up the European Monetary System (EMS), so as to make it the true precursor of monetary union. Member States agreed to pursue policies that would lead to stable balance of payments, low inflation and high levels of employment. The development of the ECU was encouraged so as to facilitate the process of economic and monetary convergence.

The Monetary Committee was established to assist in this until it is replaced by the Economic and Financial Committee in the third stage of the timetable set by the Maastricht Treaty (this is due to begin on 1 January 1999, in the event of agreement for its start date not having been met by the end of 1997). The role of the Monetary Committee is to monitor the movement of capital and 'freedom of payments' – i.e. the ease with which transactions are conducted within the Community; the goal is for this to be as easy as transactions within Member States. The Economic and Financial Committee expands on the role of the Monetary Committee by having external relations with third countries and international institutions.

THE EMS

The European Monetary System came into being after France and Germany decided to replace the 'snake' in July 1978, formally coming into operation in March 1979. The 'snake' was an agreement that all EC currencies should only move against each other by 2.25 per cent; originally they had been able to move by 2.25 per cent from their dollar parity, but this meant that the maximum swing possible was 9 per cent, because if one moved from 2.25 per cent below its dollar parity to 2.25 per cent above, and another did the reverse, then the total possible swing was 9 per cent (i.e. one went 4.5 per cent up, the other 4.5 per cent down). This was felt to be too broad, and in 1972 it was agreed that the maximum band should be 2.25 per cent in total. This band in turn was allowed to move within the 4.5 per cent boundaries of dollar parity – European currencies as a whole might swing up and down against the dollar, to a 4.5 per cent maximum, but would do so within a 2.25 per cent band against each other – so if one drew a graph of the European currencies against the dollar they would be tightly together within the parallel lines of the dollar limits, which led to the phrase 'snake in the tunnel'. Central banks were supposed to intervene to help fellow Member States stay within the band. In the event, the snake collapsed: the United Kingdom and Ireland left in 1972 after only six weeks due to an exchange crisis. Italy left in 1974, and for France it was musical chairs – out in 1974, in in 1975 and out again in 1976. Differing inflation rates between Member States had forced these countries to devalue.

In July 1978 France and Germany decided to try again – fairly stable relations between currencies were essential to the proper functioning of a fair and open common market – and devised the EMS. The first step was the formalising of the European Unit of Account (EUA) into the ECU. The EUA had been the unit used for internal Community accounting, and consisted of a weighted basket (weighted according to national share of the EU's GNP) of European currencies. These weightings were fixed as of 1 January 1993. This was an important step. Although the ECU is not in use by the public, it has assumed many of the aspects of a true currency. European banks deposit 20 per cent of their gold and dollar holdings in the European Monetary Co-operation Fund in return for ECUs. ECUs have been used now in commercial transactions and in the issuing of bonds by governments. This provides a relatively stable and immediately convertible means of exchange, and has now become the third most used currency after the US dollar and the Deutschmark in international bond issues.

Member State currencies are assigned a central rate defined by their rate of exchange with the ECU. When currencies diverge to their floor (i.e. 2.25 per cent) against another participating currency, the central banks of both currencies are *required* to intervene, buying the currency that has fallen, selling the one that has risen (the Exchange Rate Mechanism or ERM). A warning threshold for each currency is set at 75 per cent of the permitted deviation from the central rate, at which point the government of the country with the affected currency is supposed to take remedial action.

Almost immediately after the EMS came into being, it was struck by difficulties. The second oil crisis caused major disruption to European economies, with inflation being massively exacerbated in some countries; the central rate was subject to frequent revision and initially, as in any game where the rules seem to be frequently changing, annoyed some of the participants, particularly Germany which had to revalue its currency by about 12 per cent over three years against all the other currencies. The frequency of realignment slowed down thereafter, though, and to some extent the EMS can be said to have helped in the battle against inflation, as it affects government policy where exchange rates are concerned. President Mitterand of France chose to abide by EMS rules in March 1983 rather than devalue the franc, even though this led to years of austerity for the French economy – hardly what one would expect of a Socialist politician. By contrast, the United Kingdom prefers to go its own way, incapable of abiding by the discipline of the ERM and refusing to contemplate any political loss of control over the currency; this is evidenced by its refusal to countenance the setting-up of an independent central bank, despite the token greater transparency initiated by Kenneth Clarke, the United Kingdom Chancellor, in publicising how decisions are reached between the Bank of England and himself on interest rates.

THE ECU

Weighting by participating currencies

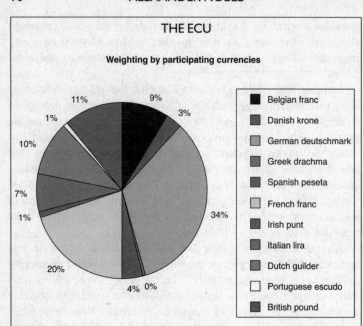

This is accurate as of 26 October 1995 – the percentages vary slightly as EU currencies move up and down against each other. The ECU (currently worth about 80–85p) is the sum of fixed amounts of its component currencies as follows:

3.431	Belgian franc
0.198	Danish krone
0.624	German Deutschmark
1.44	Greek drachma
6.885	Spanish peseta
1.332	French franc
0.009	Irish punt
151.8	Italian lira
0.219	Dutch guilder
1.393	Portuguese escudo
0.088	British pound

The Treaty of Rome concludes with some Declarations re the laying down of firmer links with member countries of the Council of Europe, movement of third-country nationals within the Community and co-operation in the war against terrorism, crime, drugs and trading in stolen works of art. Some steps have been taken towards this: international police forces co-operate routinely, though the creation of a 'Europol' centralised police force has not yet taken place. Under the Schengen Agreement, police forces were given the right to 'hot pursuit' into neighbouring EU countries, for a few kilometres at least. However, the evidence is that this has not been observed as national police forces resent incursions on to their territory, and of course France has temporarily withdrawn from Schengen.

There was also a declaration of human rights made on 5 April 1977:

> 1. The European Parliament, the Council and the Commission stress the prime importance they attach to the protection of fundamental rights as derived in particular from the constitutions of the Member States and the European Convention for the Protection of Human Rights and Fundamental Freedoms.
> 2. In the exercise of their powers and in pursuance of the aims of the European Communities they respect and will continue to respect these rights.

Interestingly, the order of declarers, so to speak, starts with the European Parliament, before the other two chief institutions. On 11 June 1986, this declaration was amplified by its specific extension to racial discrimination. This has been a growing issue in the EU, with the rise in unemployment, and the rise in immigration caused by the attraction of certain parts of the EU, particularly Germany, for third-country nationals. Also, there can be no doubt that anti-semitic and other attitudes have been on the increase in many EU countries, notably since the reunification of Germany and the Iraq war – both after the Declaration, admittedly, but the signs were already there – which led to much apprehension among some elements with regard to established Muslim communities. The Declaration is clear and comprehensive:

The European Parliament, the Council, the Representatives of the Member States, meeting within the Council, and the Commission,

Recognising the existence and growth of xenophobic attitudes, movements and acts of violence in the Community which are often directed against immigrants:

Whereas the Community institutions attach prime importance to respect for fundamental rights, as solemnly proclaimed in the Joint Declaration of 5 April 1977 [q.v.], and to the principle of freedom of movement as laid down in the Treaty of Rome;

Whereas respect for human dignity and the elimination of forms of racial discrimination are part of the common cultural and legal heritage of all the Member States;

Mindful of the positive contribution which workers who have their origins in other Member States or in third countries have made, and can continue to make, to the development of the Member State in which they legally reside and of the resulting benefits for the Community as a whole,

1. vigorously condemn all forms of intolerance, hostility and use of force against persons or groups of persons on the grounds of racial, religious, cultural, social or national differences;

2. affirm their resolve to protect the individuality and dignity of every member of society and to reject any form of segregation of foreigners;

3. look upon it as indispensable that all necessary steps be taken to guarantee that this joint resolve is carried through;

4. are determined to pursue the endeavours already made to protect the individuality and dignity of every member of society and to reject any form of segregation of foreigners;

5. stress the importance of adequate and objective information and of making all citizens aware of the dangers of racism and xenophobia and the need to ensure that all acts or forms of discrimination are prevented or curbed.

THE CECCHINI REPORT

This Report was commissioned by the EC Commission's Vice-President in 1986, Lord Cockfield, to quantify the benefits that would accrue from the establishment of a genuine single internal market. Its purpose was to spell out the implications of the 1985 White Paper, *Completing the Internal Market*. The Report was the work of teams of economists co-ordinated by Paolo Cecchini. '1992' would bring:

> Benefits most obviously for consumers and for companies in the shape of lower prices and lower costs – but benefits, also, which are stamped in social and political coinage.

It was anticipated that the benefits, derived from the enhanced competitiveness of European industry, would initially increase unemployment, but that thereafter this would decline. As mentioned elsewhere, this change in unemployment has been in one direction: up. Cecchini, to be fair, talked of a 'short-term adjustment period', and defining short term in a secular global sense is no easy task. Given global restructuring of industry – with much medium-technology industry (electrical goods, cars) and heavy industry (steel, shipbuilding) moving to low-cost countries – and the transformation of working practices in developed countries due to the so-called 'information revolution' which has hit many service jobs (e.g. bank workers are especially affected by automation, and job losses, particularly in the United Kingdom, have been high), short term should perhaps be measured in decades rather than years. After all, the original Industrial Revolution caused nearly a century of turmoil. However, the real problems are that the population has to live and suffer *now* through the period of turmoil, and this causes not only misery for individuals but misery's corollary – political and social difficulties.

The Report's genesis was the recognition that the Common Market was still a fractured market. Although progress had been successful on the elimination of tariffs and duties between individual states, there were still numerous non-tariff barriers: red tape, national standards legislation, quotas, favouring of local suppliers, subsidies etc. The elimination of these barriers would provide a supply-side shock to EC companies; i.e. their costs would be reduced if they were able to 'shop around' without impediment, but they would also have to face greater competition due to the ability of companies from other Member States to trade freely in their national markets. Greater competition would be a benefit; it would force companies to become more efficient, which would help them on global markets, and it would reduce prices for consumers and for governments (as the cost of public procurement fell). Potential gains for the EC as a whole were estimated to be ECU 174–258 billion.

Three types of barrier to free trade were identified:

1. Physical – border controls and the associated paperwork (reams of documentation were required at some customs posts, those in Italy being regarded as notorious, with queues of lorries building up – in itself a major cost).

2. Technical – national standards and product regulations. For example, the export of Leyland vans from the United Kingdom was held up in Italy because their braking systems had to be tested by the Italian authorities, and of course this meant unnecessary expense for the manufacturer, both in having to supply extra vehicles for testing and in the delay incurred before type approval. A French girder manufacturer had to wait five years for approval for its product (certification) in Germany.

3. Fiscal – divergent rates of VAT and excise duties.

The cost of border formalities to commerce was estimated to be about 2 per cent of the value of a consignment (excluding the costs to governments or, more accurately, taxpayers, of the customs controls themselves – personnel, administration, etc.) and even worse for small companies which cannot afford staff dedicated to dealing with customs formalities. It was effectively impossible for mail-order companies to operate across borders, as it was not worth their while unless they could guarantee sales in new markets of over ECU 5 million. And, not to be forgotten, there are high administrative costs (estimated by the Report to be between ECU 500 million and 1 billion), simply to maintain trade barriers – personnel at border posts and bureaucrats in government departments, solely concerned with trade restriction.

The solution proposed by the Report was a common product description and coding system (which ironically lies behind many Euromyths), a new Community tariff (TARIC) and the single administrative document (SAD).

Public spending

The Report identified public spending as being an area of major waste due to the tendency to buy national. There are three areas of loss in doing this.

1. A simple loss, known as the 'static trade effect', due to simply not being able to buy from the cheapest supplier.

2. The forgone competitive effect of domestic suppliers being forced to match external prices – 'the competition effect'.

3. The 'restructuring effect', whereby because of 2. above companies would be forced to change under the pressure of competition. This effect was of particular benefit in that its reward was that companies should become more globally competitive.

These benefits were expected to be passed on to the private sector in that many of the products it buys (computers, telephones, aeroplanes, building materials) are obviously identical to those required by the public sector. The Report estimated that these savings would be worth about ECU 17.5 billion (0.5 per cent of Community GDP in 1986). It acknowledged too that EU directives – public works (1971) and public supply contracts (1977) – on opening up public expenditure had largely been ignored by EU governments, using various excuses: strategic considerations, helping declining industries, helping new high-tech industries and for political reasons (the 'flagship industry' mentality). The recommended response was an EU-wide effort to close down the loopholes exploited by public-sector purchasers, giving interested companies legal redress to enable them to do so, and to broaden the public sector categories which came under EU legislation to include energy supplies, transport, telecommunications and water supplies.

Technical standards

The Report observed that differing national technical standards imposed pointless costs and retarded the growth of European companies. It listed these by category as follows:

Companies
— duplication of product development (a substantial proportion of R & D goes to meeting different national specifications)
— loss of potential economies of scale
— loss of competitiveness on world markets and weakness in Europe from operating on a narrow national base
Public sector purchasers
— duplication of certification and testing costs
— high prices, due to non-competitive suppliers
Consumers
— higher prices due to higher direct costs paid by companies and governments
— higher prices from less efficient companies

A Ford report estimated that the *extra cost* of getting a new car model to meet all the separate national specifications in EU Member States was ECU 286 million. Given that total sales of a new model might reach only a million, that means each car must cost the final buyer, public authority or individual, ECU 286 more than if there were EU-wide type approval. The Cecchini Report stressed the urgency of the situation, since with technology producing more and more new differing goods to new specifications, the maze of technical specifications was expanding exponentially and could only be kept under control if standards to which goods are manufactured became European. For example, differing standards such as Betamax and VHS for video recorders were seen as having reduced economies of scale and of having closed some markets; for example, in markets where one standard reached ascendancy – as did Betamax in the United States and VHS in the United Kingdom – the companies who made video recorders to the other standard were effectively excluded.

Community type-approval was agreed by the end of 1992 for motor vehicles, optional from 1 January 1993 but compulsory from 1 January 1996.

The European Committee for Standardisation (CEN – Comité Européen de Normalisation) and the European Committee for Electrotechnical Standardisation (CENELEC – as for CEN but with 'Electrotechnique' added) were seen as the ideal vehicles for setting EU standards. CEN and CENELEC consult manufacturers in the setting of standards, which in turn give them clear specifications as to which goods should comply. Products meeting these standards carry a stylised 'CE' label. Both bodies are private.

Mutual recognition

A critical issue which the Single European Act addressed particularly after the Cassis de Dijon case was a means of ensuring mutual recognition of standards, not by having identical standards everywhere but by simply stating that standards in one Member State should be recognised in another. Where states have rules, such as Germany's that the cherries in yoghurt can use beetroot colouring but not the yoghurt itself, while in Belgium you can colour the yoghurt with beetroot but not the cherries, something had to be done!

Imagine walking into a pub where the landlord gaily informs you that due to a new 'liberalising' Act of Parliament, deharmonising weights and measures, he would be happy to offer you a fifth of a pint at 50p, a quarter at 62p, a third at 81p, a half at £1.21 or any combination of these, and a pint at £2.38 depending on how rich and/or thirsty you were. Now some of us would instantly be able to calculate the cost of a pint made up of any of these sizes (£2.50, £2.48, £2.43 and £2.42 respectively) but would we know instantly whether seventh-tenths of a pint at £1.71 – a half and a fifth – was better value than two-thirds at £1.62? Probably not without a calculator, which would tell you

that the former worked out at 24.43p per tenth of a pint, the latter
at 24.3p. If the landlord continued to say that by way of
recognition of the EU, he was now also able to offer beer in metric
units, with half a litre setting you back £2.04p, you would
probably throw your hands up in despair and forswear drink. As
you walk out, you have even lost interest in whether he would
have given you short measure in the time-honoured manner.

Over time, a process of harmonisation has taken place. People
want to know the quantity as well as the quality of what they are
buying, and they want to be able to compare the value of different
quantities of any given quality almost automatically. Historically,
authorities in all countries recognised this need and tried to
standardise weights and measures, to make sure that a pint is the
same in Huddersfield as in Truro, or a decilitre the same in Cork
as in Athens.

But harmonisation in the EU is about more than just weights
and measures. It is about ensuring that a product in one country
comes up to or exceeds the national standards of the others.
Initially the approach of the Commission was to draw up
regulations which applied to every category of a product in every
country, with the ultimate aim of having its Member States
conform to those standards exactly. However, it was soon realised
that this would be a Herculean task, with teams of bureaucrats
wading through the minutiae of the product legislation of fifteen
states; instead the Gordian knot was cut, and EU legislation was
passed which stated that products reaching national standards
would be considered of an adequate standard to trade throughout
the EU – mutual recognition. This decision was reached shortly
after the well-known Cassis de Dijon case in 1979, where the
German authorities had refused to allow the import of Cassis on
the basis that it did not conform to German liquor regulations. The
European Court ruled against the Germans, as they deemed that
the French authorities were satisfied with the suitability of the
product for its purpose. British beer is in a similar position, as it is
not made according to the German *Reinheitsgebot* (the purity law)
which specifies that beer should only be made of certain ingre-
dients. Whether anybody in Germany would want to drink it is a
separate issue; it can be legally sold there under EU legislation. The

principle was adopted that as long as consumers knew what they were getting – that the constituents of any product were properly and fully labelled in a consistent fashion – then they were perfectly capable of making their own choices.

The cost of bureaucracy

The Report stated that trans-border links were severely impeded due to the different accounting standards required in different countries, with most companies having to produce at least three sets: one for their head office base, one for each country in which a subsidiary was located and another for internal management accounts. This was estimated to cause an additional 10–30 per cent cost loading to the relevant administrative departments. There were also major problems in 'transfer pricing', where part of a company supplies and charges another part for goods and services; if, for example, the engines for a car are made in Wales, to be fitted in Cologne, or if managers from France come to sort out problems in Coventry. Tax authorities often suspect that transfer pricing is used to distort a company's or its subsidiary's profits so as to minimise tax liability. Every country would aim to grab as large a slice of the tax pie as possible, which affected companies' ability to act as true multinational corporations and distorted their decision-making processes because industrial and commercial logic was swayed by tax minimisation decisions.

Additionally, difficulties are caused by the fact that in many instances companies cannot set off losses in one country against profits in another, which must deter investment. Cecchini baldly states that, 'Transfer pricing policies practised in EC countries are … so inconsistent that … a company *had* to be in an illegal situation somewhere. In fact "Europe would grind to a halt if national legislation were fully applied."' In addition to these problems companies had to face unnecessary expense in moving personnel; social security benefits are not truly portable because of differing welfare and taxation systems, and in order to ensure compliance with local national legislation companies have to pay twice, which Cecchini estimated raised mobile personnel costs by 10–15 per cent.

Service sectors

Barriers to the mobility of services were estimated to cause major costs, not just to the service sectors themselves but also to the businesses they serve. To remove them would lead to enhanced competition within the sector and wider benefits to the whole EU economy. The figure placed on the benefits to accrue would amount to ECU 22 billion (based on existing price differentials) in the financial service sector alone. A credit card balance, for example, was five times as expensive in Belgium as in the United Kingdom, while the cost of a foreign-exchange draft in Spain was over thirty-two times higher in Spain than in Belgium! Travellers' cheques, mortgages, insurance – the costs varied wildly between countries, denying consumers the benefits of competition and affecting the competitiveness of companies in different Member States through higher costs of finance.

Telecommunications was another area where European businesses faced higher costs than their United States counterparts. In the USA, for example, installing a phone line was estimated to cost $100, whereas in the EU the cost ranged from $200 to $500. Telecoms equipment was 80–100 per cent more expensive in Europe in 1980. Differing network systems due to preference being given to domestic suppliers, making equipment to national standards and requirements, led to fragmentation of the market, and the fact that PTTs (national telephone companies) were monopoly state organisations (apart from British Telecom) meant higher prices for business and consumer alike. The absence of a competitive spur meant PTTs developed their own systems for access to the integrated services digital network (ISDN). Cross-border connections were significantly higher than internal calls – i.e. to call from Ventimiglia to Nice would be more expensive than a call from Ventimiglia to Brindisi – which flies directly in the face of a single market as it simply penalises cross-border communication. Telecommunication costs affect company location decisions, as ideally they will want to originate the bulk of their calls in a low-charge country.

In sum, the Cecchini Report declared that removal of barriers would lead to major improvements in four areas:

— cost reductions, due to economies of scale and the reorganisation of business to reflect an EU 'home' market, just as American firms reflect the 'home' market of the United States.

— a reduction in prices as more efficient businesses competed more fiercely with each other. Prices for the same items across the EU varied wildly; examples given in the Report were an average of 15.2 per cent for consumer goods and 12.4 per cent for capital goods, with prices for some services such as telecoms having a 50 per cent difference. It was estimated that convergence of prices to common, low levels would lead to a 4.8 per cent boost to GDP.

— changed patterns of competition between industries, with resources being reallocated to reflect comparative advantage; this is where circumstances – whether raw materials, skilled workforce or whatever – make it more efficient to produce goods in one place rather than another. It is more sensible, for example, to produce bananas in Jamaica and export them than to grow them in Sweden, though the latter might be technically feasible. It was estimated that so-called 'indirect' gains, that is the growing efficiency of EU firms, would account for 60 per cent of the improvement in economic welfare.

— increased innovation in products and ways of doing business due to a more dynamic internal market.

The need to maintain fair competition was identified as crucial since, without doubt, companies in powerful domestic positions would continue to try to protect that position, even using government aid to do so.

A classic example of the subtlety, the apparent innocence of government protection for industry was given in the Cecchini Report: regulations which on the face of it show only environmental concern. In 1977 the Danish government banned the import of soft drinks in non-refillable containers, but the Commission ruled against this as it contravened the Treaty of Rome's provisions on free trade. To be 'fair' the Danish government then banned soft drinks and beer, whether imported or domestic, being sold in non-refillable bottles. But it is uneconomic to transport beer to a destination and then to have to pick up the empties, if that destination is over 200km away – and Denmark is a long country! Effectively therefore, German brewers were excluded from the Danish market. The inventiveness of national regulators where trade is involved should not be underestimated. Ironically, though – given how the story began, with the weight of the case against Denmark on common-market grounds – by the time a decision was made in 1988 it was accepted that Denmark was entitled to put the protection of its own environment above free trade, an indication of the growing importance the EU attaches to the environment.

Cecchini consequences

Out of the Cecchini Report came the Single Market Programme which consisted of 282 proposals, the bulk of which were passed by the deadline (though not necessarily implemented by Member States), with eighteen left of which five were considered unimportant.

In 1992 the Commission thought that about half of the EU's public contracts could be open to EU-wide suppliers, valuing the total at between ECU 240 and 340 billion. A 1989 directive set up mechanisms for suppliers to have purchasing decisions reviewed if they felt they had been unfairly treated, and in a 1990 directive water, energy, transport and telecoms were brought under the legal umbrella, with derogations (exceptions) for Spain until 1996, and Greece and Portugal until 1998. This directive specified the inclusion of supply contracts over ECU 200,000 and works contracts over ECU 5 billion. Service contracts over ECU 200,000 were covered in a directive of June 1992, and cross-border services such as refuse disposal are now carried out, for example, by French companies in the United Kingdom and British companies in the Netherlands.

CHAPTER 6

The 'Treaty of Maastricht' – The Treaty on European Union

This Treaty considerably expands the 'European idea', firming up commitments to common foreign and defence policies and emphasising the ideas of economic convergence between Member States. The Maastricht Treaty is the origin of the 'three pillars' approach to European union, whereby the original concept of the 'pillar' of economic union is expanded to embrace the 'pillar' of foreign policy and the 'pillar' of justice and home affairs. Much of what was outlined in the Treaty of Rome, as amended by the various subsequent Treaties, is reiterated, with more recent concerns taken into account (e.g. 'sustainable' economic growth) and moving from setting up a Social Fund to developing policies under which it will operate. It is also specific in its determination to encourage the development of trans-European networks. 'Consumer protection' is specifically recognised as an issue, though it was implicit in the provisions of the Treaty of Rome. It also states that Member States' culture, health protection, civil protection, energy and tourism will become concerns of the Union.

Article 3a specifies steps towards economic union:

> ... the adoption of an economic policy which is based on the close co-ordination of Member States' economic policies ... on the definition of common objectives ...,

and proceeds to outline one of the most controversial policy statements in its second clause:

> ... these activities shall include the *irrevocable* fixing of exchange rates leading to the introduction of a single currency, the ECU, and the definition of a single monetary policy and exchange rate policy, the primary objective of both shall be to maintain price stability and ... to support the general economic policies of the Community ...

To date, European countries are still arguing about the name of the currency. ECU may be an acronym (in English) for European Currency Unit, but it is also an old French coin, the *écu*, and national prejudices – a primitive belief in the sanctity of a name, whatever its origin – have led to protest. Also the ERM (exchange-rate mechanism), with its two bands, has to tread a difficult path between being flexible enough to include all Euro-currencies, while being tight enough to actually mean something with regard to convergence. As we all know, in September 1992 the United Kingdom found its currency unable to remain even within the more flexible band, and Italy followed shortly thereafter. Spain and its main trading partner, Portugal, had to withdraw in 1995 as the peseta crashed. When these currencies will be stable enough to rejoin the ERM is a moot point; moreover there are very real problems even if they do. One of the problems of agreeing exchange rates is that most national governments have their own agenda with regard to their currency, an agenda that changes with domestic political and economic requirements. For example, if one government is determined to increase imports, lowering the exchange rate will make its goods more attractive; or one might want to reduce import costs (in which case a higher exchange rate is preferable); or internal policies, such as cooling a period of expansion and possibly accelerated inflation, can lead a government to set higher interest rates in order to cut down investment and/or consumer demand. Countries with high unemployment generally would like to cut their interest rates, so as to boost their economies, but this can make their currencies unacceptably weak. The definition of 'unacceptably' is not precise – they can be unacceptable to one's trading partners because they tilt the export/import balance in one's favour, or because of national pride or a host of other reasons.

Provisional phasing of the introduction of the ECU (or whatever it is finally called) is set out below. It should be noted that some Member States, notably the United Kingdom, have argued that the ECU should act as a parallel currency, not a replacement. From the EU's perspective, it would have to hope that 'good money drives out bad', and this might well be the case as citizens of countries with traditionally weak currencies switch into ECUs, just as the Russians use the US dollar.

PHASES OF EUROPEAN MONETARY UNION

Phase one	Phase two	Phase three
Participants announced	Exchange rates fixed	ECU notes and coins introduced
EMU start date fixed	ECU enters use	Banks complete retail systems changeover
Deadline for final switch to single currency announced	Monetary and exchange-rate policy to be in ECUs	National currencies withdrawn
ECSB and ECB begin operations	Interbank, monetary, capital and exchange markets in ECUs	Public and private operators switch to ECUs
Production of ECU notes and coins	New government debt to be in ECUs	ECU becomes sole currency

To resume the story of the currency crashes, the broad band was increased to 15 per cent in 1993 to accommodate the devaluers, but this band is so broad as to make the notion of convergence implausible.

Subsidiarity is the next new concept introduced in the Maastricht Treaty. The Community is supposed to limit its actions to the objectives assigned to it by the Treaty, and Article 3b states:

> In areas which do not fall within its exclusive competence, the Community shall take action, in accordance with the principle of subsidiarity, only if and in so far as the objectives of the proposed action cannot be sufficiently achieved by the Member States and can, therefore, by reason of the scale or effects of the proposed action, be better achieved by the Community.

In theory this is perfectly clear. The Community will not interfere where to do so confers no advantage. But it is not so easy to separate issues which are best ordered by the Community rather than a Member State, and Member States have shown some reluctance in defining which issues are better dealt with by the Community. There is a natural aversion to relinquishing what to date have been regarded as national interests, and to subsume these in the interest of a greater good which in effect is largely dictated from outside (even though, of course, all Member States have a say in those decisions, but may end up being outvoted). However, there is a practical basis to encouraging subsidiarity on the EU's part. The Commission is heavily overworked, and the more decisions it can devolve the more efficient and responsive it can become.

Article 4a states that a European System of Central Banks (ECSB) and a European Central Bank (ECB) will be established. The role of the latter is to promote monetary union, and it alone will have the right to authorise the printing of a common European currency.

Citizenship was established in the Union, whereby every national of a Member State becomes a citizen of the Union, and the Council can with unanimous agreement work towards making this a reality, in terms of freedom of movement, if the European Parliament agrees. One concrete example of the rights of the EU citizen is that of voting or standing in municipal elections, or in elections to the European Parliament in the state in which he or she resides, with derogations (exceptions) for Member States with particular problems. EU citizens can call on the protection of diplomatic or consular services of other Member States when in third countries; they also have the right to petition the European

Parliament or to apply to the recently appointed European Ombudsman, Jacob Magnus Søderman. Under the terms of the Treaty, the Council can go beyond provisions of the Treaty in adding to and strengthening these rights where unanimity is achieved.

Maastricht then leaves much of the Treaty of Rome unamended, until the provisions on movement of capital are reached in Article 73, where the right to apply national laws with regard to the taxes and capital of residents and non-residents is recognised, as is the national right to supervise its financial institutions or to require declaration of capital movements. Member States can also act unilaterally with regard to capital movements to third countries, but the measures they take must gain the retrospective approval of the Council by qualified majority if they are not to be amended or abolished. The Community can also take general action via the Council (on a qualified majority) on a proposal from the Commission, and after consulting the ECB where capital movements by a third country threaten the path to monetary union.

Liberalisation of payments, whereby creditors can be paid in their national currency, is established as being essential to the free movement of goods, services and capital. The Member States all agree to reduce any restrictions caused by current cash movement that limit the achievement of free trade (Article 73h).

In Article 75, relating to transport policy, the change is that proposals with regard to transport come under the provisions of Article 189c (see under 'Revisions to the Institutions of the Community', pp. 124–5).

Article 92 is changed to add 'aid to promote culture and heritage conservation where such aid does not affect trading conditions and competition in the Community to an extent that is contrary to the common interest'. This article shows the expanding awareness of the EU of issues affecting the Union outside the economic, as it gradually seeks to apply EU-wide policies; concern about culture has grown as states have seen much of their heritage swamped by development, and the EU is aware too that individual states have shown anxiety about preserving the cultural traditions which they believe make them different. In the

United Kingdom, the EU has been presented by Prime Minister Major (summer 1995) as being a threat to 'warm beer and cricket'. Jacques Santer pointed out that the EU has not the slightest intention of interfering with these (rather dubious?) pleasures. More importantly, though, the EU has given grants to arts initiatives and to such projects as the restoration of buildings of historical and architectural interest. The European Youth Orchestra, for example, gets ECU 400,000 per annum from the EU, and the Merseyside Development Corporation received £35 million from the EU (as against £28 million from the United Kingdom government and £28 million from the private sector).

Article 100c states that the Council, acting unanimously, on a proposal from the Commission and in consultation with the European Parliament, shall decide which third country nationals need visas to enter the EU. From 1 January 1996 the Council will act on a qualified majority on this issue. Article 100 also provides for emergency visa introduction in the event of the unexpected influx of a large number of third-country nationals into the EU. Individual states can also apply to the Commission for proposals in this area. The Co-ordinating Committee, consisting of as yet undefined 'senior officials', presumably Member State government appointees, is to help the Council in making its decisions.

The Council is given responsibility in Article 103 for the drafting of broad guidelines for the economic policies of the Member States, and it is stated that Member States recognise that their economic policies are of common interest. The Council has to report on this to the European Council, which is expected to come up with a finalised version of the guidelines, whereupon the Council will inform the European Parliament as to what has been decided. The Commission is to keep the Council informed as to economic developments in individual states for the purposes of monitoring and assessing progress towards convergence. Where Member States seem to be diverging from the goal of economic and monetary union, the Council – acting on a qualified majority on the recommendation of the Commission – may make recommendations to that state and make these public under the same conditions. The President of the Council and the Commission have to report to the European Parliament on the results of their monitoring and assessment, and the President can be asked to appear before the relevant Committee of the European Parliament in the event that the recommendations have been made public, to explain the Council's rationale.

Within the framework of the Treaty the Council can, unanimously, decide on appropriate measures during periods of economic difficulty, particularly where the supply of certain products is affected. If a Member State is in difficulty the Council can, unanimously, on a Commission proposal, give financial help to that state. In the case of natural disasters, only a qualified majority is needed. The President of the Council must inform the European Parliament as to what has been decided.

In Article 104, overdrafts with the ECB or with Member State central banks are banned for Community institutions or central, regional or local government or any other public undertakings, nor can they sell bonds to the ECB or national central banks. This does not apply to publicly owned credit institutions which are involved in the supply of reserves to central banks. Article 104a bans privileged access by the same institutions to other financial institutions. Definitions of the various bodies were to be prepared by the Council by 1 January 1994 and these were completed and approved by the Council and the European Parliament by the end of December 1993. In Article 104b it is made clear that the Community will not be liable in joint projects for the commitments of other parties – central governments, public authorities or Member States – nor shall Member States be liable for other Member States, except where specific guarantees have been given.

In line with the commitment to a single currency, it was agreed in Article 104c that Member States would try to bring the ratio of the deficit in government spending to gross domestic product (GDP) within certain parameters – 3 per cent for the planned deficit, and 60 per cent for government spending as a whole. This means that a government should not plan for government borrowing to exceed 3 per cent of GDP, or that total cumulative national debt should exceed 60 per cent of GDP. Not all Member States have been able to observe these criteria; Italy and Belgium in particular are offenders, having very high national debts. Even Germany – since the government investment requirements caused by reunification – has strayed beyond the limits. It is initially the Commission's responsibility to monitor the situation and to prepare a report for the Council, in consultation with the Monetary Committee set up by Article 109c of the Maastricht Treaty. If the Commission believes that there is, or there is the risk of, an excessive deficit it passes on this opinion to the Council which then, after listening to the relevant Member State, can make recommendations to that state based on those of the Commission, for which a qualified majority is required. This qualified majority excludes the votes of the Member State under scrutiny. If the state concerned does not act within a certain time, the Council will make its recommendations public. The sanctions the Council can employ to enforce compliance are as follows:

(a) it can require the Member State concerned to publish more information when issuing bonds or securities;

(b) it can ask the European Investment Bank (EIB) to reconsider its lending policy to the Member State;

(c) it can require the Member State concerned to make a *non-interest bearing* deposit with the Community until the deficit is corrected in the Council's view;

(d) it can impose fines.

The President of the Council has to inform the European Parliament of any measures decided.

These sanctions are of increasing severity; (a) is an embarrassment, in that effectively it requires a government to justify the reasons for the issue – as a generalisation, where public deficits are concerned the Commission takes a kinder view of deficits for investment purposes; (b) is a potential loss to the state concerned; (c) is a definite loss, because normally a state could expect interest on its deposits, and the period during which the deposit is with the Community is of indefinite length; and (d) is self-explanatory. These provisions give the Commission and Council a very real say in the economic and financial policies of Member States.

As soon as a Member State is deemed to have complied, the Council undertakes to make a public statement to that effect.

The Maastricht Treaty also set up the ESCB, the European

System of Central Banks, whose primary role is to assure price stability within the Community. Its remit is similar to that of the Bundesbank in Germany, with responsibilities including defining and implementing Community monetary policy, conducting foreign-exchange operations, and holding and managing the foreign reserves of Member States (apart from what are described as 'foreign-exchange working balances', i.e. day-to-day foreign-exchange holdings of which Member States retain control). The ESCB – as well as working with the European Central Bank (ECB), whose future establishment was laid down in the Treaty, and having the ECB as a member – assumed interim responsibility for areas which the ECB will take over once the latter's full role is defined by the Council, with the assent of the European Parliament being granted. Some powers were granted to the ECB from the start. It has the sole right to authorise the issue of bank notes within the Community, whether issued by itself or by national central banks. The Treaty also declares: 'The bank notes issued by the ECB and the national central banks shall be the only such notes to have the status of legal tender within the Community.' Member States can also issue coins subject to ECB approval. The Governing Council and the Executive Board of the ECB govern the ESCB, so though the ECB's role is not fully defined it will clearly participate, via the ESCB, in formulating it. Article 107 makes it clear that the ECB and the ESCB, like the Bundesbank, shall be fully independent of any outside party, whether they be Community institutions or Member State governments.

The ECB has been given the right, just as the Commission has in its areas of competence, to make regulations, to take decisions in accordance with the ESCB statute, to make recommendations and give opinions. These different degrees of ordinance parallel those of the Commission (see pp. 63–4) in their degree of compulsion. The ECB will also be able to impose fines or periodic penalty payments on those who do not obey its regulations and decisions.

The Treaty also makes provision for the Council – acting unanimously on a recommendation from the ECB or the Commission, and with the assent of the European Parliament – to agree an exchange-rate system for the ECU in relation to non-Community currencies. This is primarily to bring future

Community members' currencies into a stable embracing system, that will make accession easier, as it will have involved a degree of currency convergence. For example, the Swedish krona tracked the deutschmark for a period before Sweden's EU membership, so as to keep the krona within the tight exchange-rate mechanism (ERM) criterion; ultimately it had to devalue, but the intention was there. Such convergence would make it easier – were Poland and the Czech Republic to enter the Community – for the zloty or the Czech crown to be swiftly subsumed into a single currency. The Council can also adjust the relationships of currencies within the ERM, subject to consulting the ECB and on a Commission recommendation, and can make agreements with other countries not inside any ERM re exchange rates; the Commission is to be closely involved in all negotiations, and the intention is to present a single Community front. These agreements are binding on all Community institutions.

The Governing Council of the ECB is to be composed of the Executive Board, consisting of the President, the Vice-President and four other members, and the Governors of Member State national banks. The appointment of the Executive Board is by the heads of state or government, on the recommendation of the Council after it has consulted the European Parliament and the Governing Council of the ECB; the term of office will be eight years, not renewable. The ECB has to prepare an annual report on the activities of the ESCB in the current and previous year for the European Parliament, the Council and the Commission. The European Parliament can debate the report.

Maastricht also contains several transitional provisions (apart from the Monetary Committee) outlined earlier under Chapter 3, 'Competition Policy', p. 40. In Article 109e it is specified that Member States will if necessary adopt programmes to accelerate economic convergence, and the implementation of Community law regarding the internal market; reference is made, in particular, 'with regard to price stability and sound public finances'. This was to be done before 1 January 1994, the beginning of the second stage of achieving economic and monetary union. As we know, this has not been achieved and the other target dates are likely to slip back. There is talk of the third stage not being started in time, even by the 1999 fall-back date. Two possible outcomes are increasingly discussed: (i) a fast-track Europe, whereby France, Germany and the Benelux countries form a 'core' with a single currency and a more homogenous economic outlook – countries such as Britain, Italy and Spain would be left outside this, catching up when they can; and (ii) a simple failure to achieve a single currency. Even (i) looks less likely than it did. Germany, the Netherlands and Luxembourg are financially sound and, as discussed earlier, any of their national currencies are accepted near their borders (Luxembourg shops even price goods in ECUs!), but some German opinion is growingly increasingly averse to tying the mark to what it regards as the weak currencies of Europe, and there is some doubt as to how long France can maintain its *'franc fort'* policy given the strains caused by being adjacent to Spain and Italy, both of whose currencies have undergone competitive devaluation. And no country would intentionally fix its currency to an ECU if it felt its economic circumstances were about to change. Still, as discussed earlier, the advance of electronics – where value is transferred down telephone lines, and issued in the form of credit or bank notes – makes the arguments of politicians increasingly old-fashioned. Computer bytes do not have names or the faces of national figures printed upon them. It is such electronic transfers that have the potential to cut transaction costs, as the real cost of effecting them is measured in microvolts. Furthermore, the internationalisation of business organisation means that commercial pressures will become more important than political and nationalistic considerations. As so often, politicians are well behind technological and commercial developments in their deliberations.

The Treaty also set up the European Monetary Institute (EMI), managed by a Council consisting of a President and the Governors of the national central banks, one of whom is the Vice-President. Initially the President was chosen on the recommendation of the Committee of Governors (of the central banks), with the agreement of the heads of state, though in future the Council will make this recommendation. The Council appoints the Vice-President. The EMI's role is to prepare the ground for a single monetary policy, specifically to:

— strengthen co-operation between the national central banks;
— strengthen the co-ordination of monetary policies of the Member States, with the aim of ensuring price stability;
— hold consultations concerning issues falling within the competence of the national central banks and affecting the stability of financial institutions and markets;
— take over the tasks of the European Monetary Co-operation Fund, which shall be dissolved . . .
— facilitate the use of the ECU and oversee its development, including the smooth functioning of the ECU clearing system.

Before the third stage begins it is expected to:

— prepare the instruments and procedures necessary for carrying out a single monetary policy in the third stage;
— promote the harmonisation, where necessary, of rules and practices governing the collection, compilation and distribution of statistics in the areas within its field of competence;
— prepare the rules for operations to be undertaken by the national central banks within the framework of the ESCB;
— promote the efficiency of the [sic] cross-border payments;
— supervise the technical preparation of ECU bank notes.

This is quite an extensive programme, even if framed in few words, and on top of this the EMI is supposed to formalise the role and structure of the ESCB by 31 December 1996.

The EMI, with the Commission, has to report to the Council on progress made towards economic convergence. The criteria include low inflation, which is measured against the average of the three best-performing Member States being a maximum of 1.5 per cent higher over a year; low governments deficits, staying within the bands of the ERM (4.5 per cent for narrow band, 2.25 per cent either side of the central rate, 15 per cent for wide band), for over two years; and long-term interest rates which are no more than 2 per cent higher than the average of the best-performing states. The Council then has to decide – acting by a qualified majority on a recommendation from the Commission – whether each Member State has attained the conditions for a single currency and whether a majority has reached them, and then whether it is appropriate to enter the third stage. In any event the Council has to meet before 1 July 1998 to confirm by qualified majority which Member States fulfil the necessary conditions for adopting a single currency. There is to be an Intergovernmental Conference (IGC) in 1996 which will discuss these issues, but there is no guarantee that they will recommend starting the third stage before the deadline of 1 January 1999. The situation with regard to Member States that are not part of the single currency is supposed to be reviewed at least once every two years. Such states are known as 'Member States with derogation' and they do not share in the ESCB's deliberations. The first board of the ECB will be appointed on 1 July 1998 at the latest by Member States without a derogation. Currently London and Frankfurt are in contention as to which will provide the location for the ECB, but London's chances are severely limited by the tepid attitude towards a single currency of the Conservative Party currently in power in the United Kingdom. Once the ECB has been established, the EMI will cease to function. The only influence Member States with a derogation will have is that they form part of a secondary governing council (Article 45 of the Statute of the ESCB).

When the third stage begins the Council shall, after consulting the ECB and with unanimous agreement from the Member States without derogation, fix the exchange rate of their currencies with the ECU, and it shall be introduced into those countries as soon as possible.

A new chapter – 'Education, Vocational Training and Youth' – was added to social policy in the Maastricht Treaty. This chapter is sensitive to the desire of Member States to carry out their own programmes in fulfilling its requirements; in recommending action the Community fully respects 'the responsibility of Member States for the content of teaching and the organisation of education systems and their cultural and linguistic diversity'.

The emphasis on 'European-ness' was vastly increased, with a

'European dimension' being specified as part of education, and with academic exchanges and mutual recognition of qualifications being recommended within the Community and with outside bodies, especially the Council of Europe. Vocational training was also given increased importance, in particular for the young, with Community programmes to run alongside those in Member States. Youth training was emphasised because of the disproportionate effect of unemployment on young people, who simply fail to enter the world of employment on leaving school or tertiary education. It is recognised within the Community, as well as by the G7 countries, that employment statistics do not reflect youth unemployment which is often double or more that of adult unemployment. The agricultural workforce is specifically mentioned in Article 130e to be a subject for such programmes.

Maastricht also emphasises the diversity as well as the common interests of Member States. A new Title IX was added, replacing the previous Article 128:

> The Community shall contribute to the flowering of the cultures of the Member States, while respecting their national and regional diversity and at the same time bringing the common cultural heritage to the fore.

Areas such as conservation and preservation of the cultural heritage are cited, as the Community stakes its claim to operate outside purely economic fields. Titles X and XI are also new in that they are more specific than the provisions of the Treaty of Rome, though the same concerns were expressed in that Treaty. Title X, 'Public Health', expresses the Community's desire to fight against major diseases, including drug dependence, in a co-ordinated way, and to develop common programmes together with third countries. Future policy-making is to take both cultural and health considerations into account. Title XI, 'Consumer Protection', declares the Community's willingness to ensure higher standards in consumer information with regard to health, safety and value.

THE COHESION FUND

The Cohesion Fund was also formalised by the Treaty of Maastricht. The purpose of this fund is to bring the economies of the four poorest EU countries up to speed before monetary union (Greece, Spain, Ireland and Portugal) and to help those countries, specifically in transport and environmental investment. Projects – unlike those for the Structural Funds, which take regional interests into account – are agreed between the Commission and the Member State. The criteria are more generous than for the Structural Funds, as the Cohesion Fund will provide up to 85 per cent of the cost of a project, and where the Commission has initiated a project it will pay the entire preparatory costs. The Cohesion Fund began operations in 1993 (its formal inception was May 1994) and assisted its target countries with ECU 1.5 billion. Spain received the lion's share with 55 per cent, Portugal received 18 per cent, Greece 18 per cent and Ireland 9 per cent. The total amount available between 1993 and 1999 is ECU 15 billion.

Transport policy received a shot in the arm with Title XII, 'Trans-European Networks'. By the time that Maastricht was signed it was recognised that the only way to truly shrink distances in Europe and to increase the efficiency and availability of transport, telecommunications and energy infrastructure was to set up a specific programme. To bring outlying regions into proper contact with the rest of the Community – and hence to spread economic opportunity – a planned cohesive structure was necessary. Also in the world of telecommunications, growing competition from the United States and Japan means that Europe has to adopt common standards in order to compete, rather than continue with what are now regarded as small national markets. The GSM standard for mobile phones was developed by the Community, and new road and rail networks are planned under Community auspices. Member States have a high degree of involvement in these programmes, as obviously they affect them territorially. The goal of standards covering a broader range of communications is set out in Title XII; the problem with the older forms of network, particularly railways as discussed earlier, is that the existing infrastructure would be extremely expensive to replace, partly because much of it has been amortised (e.g. railway buildings) and would have to be replaced from scratch. But standards in road development and electronic communications will be easier to attain, partly because most Member States have road programmes (both new and improvements), and in electronics the field is so new that standards can be defined at the outset of development programmes. Where a project is of common interest – that is, it improves communications between two states – the Community may offer financial support through the Cohesion Fund with the proviso that the project be economically viable. The Treaty also states that interoperability is an important criterion for projects. The adoption of energy standards would also lead to more efficient use of energy as the peaks and troughs of national or regional demand can be smoothed out by exporting energy (as Electricité de France does to the United Kingdom) and by improving energy supply to outlying regions, so that their competitiveness can be improved.

Title XII, 'Industry', replaces Article 130 of the Treaty of Rome with a commitment to ensuring that Community industries are competitive, with particular reference (inserted at Mrs Thatcher's insistence) to benefiting small and medium-sized enterprises (SMEs), and in 130a rural areas are added to least-favoured regions as targets for reducing regional disparities in levels of development. The Commission has to report to the European Parliament, the Council, the Economic and Social Committee and the Committee of the Regions every three years on the progress made in achieving economic and social cohesion.

'Research and Technological Development', Title XV, does not add much to the amended Treaty of Rome, apart from mentioning that projects should be of 'high quality' (one wonders what they were before!) and that instead of Member States simply liaising with the Commission in such activities, they should co-ordinate their activities with the Community so that both are mutually consistent. Also it is established that a multi-annual framework programme does exist and the Council can adopt its constituent programmes after receiving a proposal from the Commission and consulting the European Parliament and the Economic and Social Committee.

Programmes are to have cost ceilings set before commencement.

In Title XVI, 'Environment', Article 130r is supplemented by an important fourth clause which sets the objective of: 'promoting measures at international level to deal with regional or worldwide environmental policies'. It is recognised that pollution knows no borders and that where, for example, poorer nations have serious environmental problems, which may or may not affect their neighbours, then richer nations have to step in with financial help and technical expertise. The obvious example of this is Chernobyl, where the break-up of the former Soviet Union led to economic chaos and an inability to fund the work needed to make the reactors safe; indeed the original 'sarcophagus' over the exploded reactor is deemed to need repair, and meanwhile three identical reactors continue to operate because Ukraine is too poor to replace them or buy alternative energy supplies. The pollution however spread over all of Europe, to the outer limits.

The Council also adopted a more specific role in Member States' internal affairs with regard to the environment. Article 130s states that the Council, acting unanimously, shall adopt:

— provisions primarily of a fiscal nature;
— measures concerning town and country planning, land use with the exception of waste management, and measures of a general nature, and management of water resources;
— measures significantly affecting a Member State's choice between different energy sources and the general structure of its water supply.

This is a significant, if unheralded, expansion of the Council's role in Member States' affairs. The first clause means such things as a carbon tax, to reduce pollution and increase efficient energy use. This would be EU-wide and at the time of writing has met with resistance, primarily from the United Kingdom which has vetoed its adoption. The planning measures have not as yet been defined, nor has land use. Water resources are specifically mentioned for a number of reasons: water is supplied for drinking; it is much used by industry and also for transport; and many rivers such as the Rhine or Meuse/Maas (depending on whether you are in France or the Netherlands) run through several countries, and therefore are of proper interest to the EU. Member States are to pay for the environment policy, though where it is difficult for a Member State to comply – basically, if it is one of the poorer countries – the Council can allocate funds from the Cohesion Fund.

Title XVII, 'Development Co-operation', brings aid to developing countries into the EU's remit, complementing the efforts of individual Member States, and specifies that it is to be devoted to 'sustainable economic and social development in developing countries', their integration into the world economy and a campaign against poverty. It is to be conducted with a view to 'developing and consolidating democracy and the rule of law, and to that of respecting human rights and fundamental freedoms', and working with the UN and other international bodies. The EIB is the EU's instrument for donating economic assistance.

REVISIONS TO THE INSTITUTIONS OF THE COMMUNITY

The Treaty on European Union took steps to reduce the 'democratic deficit'. It refers in Article 137 simply to the European Parliament's 'powers' rather than the much-qualified 'advisory and supervisory powers'. These powers have been expanded by the 'co-decision procedure' to include the rejection of Council 'common positions' in the following areas: free movement of workers, the single market, education, research, the environment, TENs, health, culture and consumer protection. If the 'conciliation procedure' (see below) fails, then the European Parliament can reject the Council's initiatives. The European Parliament was also given the right to set up Committees of Enquiry where at least 25 per cent of its members think that Community law has been infringed, except where such infringements are already before a court of law. Citizens, residents and persons working in any Member State also have a right to petition the European Parliament where they are affected in any area coming under the Community's competence. An Ombudsman was also appointed to whom the same rights of petition exist, re maladministration by Community institutions, apart from the Court of Justice and Court of First Instance. The Council also received a General Secretariat, based in Luxembourg, to assist with its increasing workload.

Further attempts to reduce the democratic deficit and to increase the transparency of decision-making were included in the declarations attached to the Treaty on European Union. Declaration 13 encourages the dialogue between national parliaments and the European Parliament, specifically mentioning that national parliaments should have information about Commission proposals in good time, and in Declaration 14 a Conference of Parliaments is invited to gather for consultative purposes. There is a widespread awareness that the European Parliament and national parliaments have tended to operate as parallel non-communicative organisations rather than as parts of a cohesive political system; their roles should properly be complementary. Furthermore, the Maastricht participants recognised that the Commission would inspire more public confidence if the public had information about the decision-making process (Declaration 17), and that the Commission should report to the Council on this by 1993. The steps the Commission took were to publish its annual legislative programme at an earlier stage so as to allow more opportunity for discussion, and to make greater use of 'green papers' – essentially discussion documents for proposed policies, which when decisions have been made become 'white papers', the final texts of which are voted on. In October 1993 the Council, the Commission and the European Parliament confirmed their continued commitment to transparency. The Council has taken steps to open some of its meetings to the public, and to publish its common position on issues and how votes were cast. In October 1995, more transparency was prised out of it by the *Guardian* newspaper which, with the assistance of the Danish and Swedish governments, won a case at the European Court of Justice which ruled that the Council was wrong to deny a journalist access to minutes of three of its meetings. Also, in the same month, the Council independently drew up a new code of conduct giving broader public access to its procedures.

Article 158 introduced an important change, namely that the European Parliament was given the right of approval of the whole of the Commission, whose period of office was now increased to five years. Jacques Santer was the first President of the

Commission to have to undergo this new process, and in the event he was only narrowly approved by a margin of 22 (260 for, 238 against and 23 abstentions).

The Court of First Instance was formalised in Article 168a. It does not determine points of EU law, which still remains the province of the Court of Justice, but it can hear certain classes of action, subject to appeal only on points of law. This reduces the workload of the Court of Justice, since on issues where EU law is established the Court of First Instance can decide on a case. Article 171 amplifies the Court of Justice's means of enforcement, by specifying that the Commission is to monitor compliance with its judgements, and in cases where a Member State does not comply within a certain time, it can specify the amount that that Member State must pay. Articles 175 to 184 extend the Court of Justice's jurisdiction to cover the ECB and the ESCB.

CHANGES TO LEGISLATIVE PROCEDURE

Article 189 as replaced by the Treaty of Maastricht is extremely important as it adds the European Parliament to the Council: '*the European Parliament acting jointly with the Council* [author's italics], the Council and Commission shall make regulations and issue directives, take decisions, make recommendations or deliver opinions'. Article 190 adds 'European Parliament' to the Council and Commission, where the requirement for openness in giving reasons for legislation: Article 191 requires that regulations, directives and decisions are signed by both the President of the Council *and* the President of the European Parliament. Articles 189a, 189b and 189c are also very important in that they set out the decision-making process. Much of the original Treaty of Rome spelled out the decision-making process for each clause in its entirety. Maastricht took the rational approach of incorporating all this into two articles which are then referred to in Articles where they apply, rather than repeating it throughout. This neatly removed the need to insert in every relevant clause of the Treaty of Rome the adjustments that had been made to the process, mostly in favour of qualified majorities rather than unanimity and giving an increased role to the European Parliament.

Article 189a defines the procedure whereby the Council requires unanimity to alter a proposal from the Commission, subject to the 'Conciliation Committee' (see below).

The 'co-decision' procedure

The procedure outlined in 189b is as follows: the Commission submits proposals to *the European Parliament and* the Council. The Council adopts what is known as a 'common position' by qualified majority, *'after obtaining the opinion of the European Parliament'*. The European Parliament – having been informed of this common position, and the full reasons for its adoption – then has four courses of action, to be undertaken within three months:

(a) approve the common position in which case the Council can confirm it as an act.

(b) not come to a decision, in which case the Council can confirm the common position as an act.

(c) inform the Council that it intends to reject the common position by an absolute majority, in which case the Council *may* convene the Conciliation Committee, a new institution set up by the Maastricht Treaty. After the Council has further explained its position to the Conciliation Committee, the European Parliament can then confirm that it intends to reject the common position by an absolute majority or propose amendments.

(d) propose amendments to the common position by an absolute majority, which are then put to the Council and Commission for their opinions.

Such amendments are forwarded to the Council and Commission for their opinions. If within three months the Council agrees to the amendments, then the act shall be adopted according to the modified common position. If however the Commission is against the amendments, then the Council has to approve them unanimously. If the *Council* does not agree the amendments, then the Presidents of the Council and of the European Parliament can immediately convene the Conciliation Committee. This Committee is composed of equal numbers of representatives or members of the Council and of representatives of the European Parliament. The Commission is allowed to take part in the deliberations of the Committee and has a duty to act to bring the two parties together. Where the Conciliation Committee is able to come to agreement on the text of an act within six weeks, the Council by a qualified majority and the European Parliament by an absolute majority can adopt the revised text, again if they vote within six weeks of receiving the revised text. If either party does not approve within that period, then the act is considered not to have been adopted.

If the Conciliation Committee fails to reach agreement, the Council can, by a qualified majority, re-present its original text, or if it so desires with the amendments originally proposed by the European Parliament, within six weeks of the Committee's time period having expired. The European Parliament then has another six weeks in which to reject the proposed act by absolute majority. The chances of any proposed act getting through at this stage are slim, and to allow proper debate the initial three months' approval period can be extended by a month and the period allowed to the Conciliation Committee can be extended by two weeks, where the Council and European Parliament agree. In the event of the European Parliament acting as described in (c) above, the three-month period is automatically extended by two months.

The 'co-operation' procedure

Article 189c is slightly different, and applies where the Commission has presented a proposal, just to the Council, which after consulting the *opinion* of the EP (i.e. the proposal is not presented to the European Parliament by the Commission), adopts a common position. The procedure is then similar to 189b, except that if the position is rejected the Council needs unanimity to re-present the common position where the European Parliament has rejected it. Where amendments are proposed, it is up to the Commission to review the common position with reference to the European Parliament's suggestions, and if it throws out some of these amendments then they can only be adopted by a unanimous Council. It also requires unanimity on the Council's part to amend in turn the Commission's amendments, but only a qualified majority to accept a proposal as revised by the Commission. The Council has to act within three months, in the event of the European Parliament rejecting or amending a proposal. If it fails to do so, then the proposal is dropped, though again, as in 189b, the Council and European Parliament can agree to extend this period by one month.

Chapter 4 of the Treaty establishes 'The Committee of the Regions'. This comprises representatives from regional and local bodies, and the Member States send the following numbers:

Belgium	12
Denmark	9
Germany	24
Greece	12
Spain	21
France	24
Ireland	9
Italy	24
Luxembourg	6
Netherlands	12
Austria	12
Portugal	12
Finland	9
Sweden	12
United Kingdom	24

This is a consultative body, supposedly independent of outside interests, with Community action as its priority. The role of the Committee is similar to that of EcoSoc, but for regional policy; the Commission is very concerned with bringing the regions 'closer' to the centre – i.e. ensuring they share the benefits of the EU – and regional policy is by no means peripheral.

The Committee of the Regions describes itself as the 'Champion of subsidiarity'; the representatives are regional presidents, mayors of cities and chairmen of city and county councils. The idea behind forming the Committee was that it should comprise those closely involved with local government, as they would have a clear idea of how the EU's policies affect the ordinary citizen. It had its first session in March 1994, since when it has tackled such issues as guidelines for a trans-European airport network, rural tourism development and Europe's march towards becoming an information society.

Article 198e of the Maastricht Treaty indicates that the EIB is supposed to co-ordinate its activities with the Structural Funds and 'other Community Financial Instruments'.

Title II, 'Financial Provisions', extended the budget to cover administrative costs for areas into which the EU had expanded under the Treaty, namely common foreign and security policy and co-operation in the fields of justice and home affairs (e.g. such initiatives as Europol). Article 201 updates the Treaty of Rome to include the Council's decision on 'own resources' – from which the budget must be funded – of 7 May 1985. 'Own resources' were unfinalised at the time the Treaty of Rome was signed.

The current system of 'own resources' was laid down in a Council Decision in June 1988, which was retroactively applied from 1 February 1989 to 1 January 1988. Previously the EU had three types of revenue source, but these were now increased to four:

1. The Common External Tariff, the tariff on imports to the EU, which have dwindled over the years, and duties still applicable under the ECSC.

2. Agricultural levies under the CAP on EU imports.

3. 1.4 per cent of Member States' VAT revenue. The base for this is assessed in a 'uniform manner' with the proviso that it shall not account for more than 55 per cent of a Member State's GNP. This proviso is to protect poorer states. The Commission had hoped for 2 per cent, but this was the level set at the Fontainebleau European Council of 1984.

4. A GNP-related contribution assessed annually. This ensures that part of Member States' contribution is according to their means.

The agreed maximum that all these can account for is no more than 1.27 per cent of EU Member States' GNP during the 1993–99 period (previously 1.2 per cent).

The Commission additionally undertakes in Article 201a not to put forward proposals that cause its commitments to go beyond the agreed budget. The European Parliament, on a recommendation from a qualified majority from the Council, gives the Commission its discharge (i.e. approval) for the budget, though it and the Council examine the budget and pass comments on how it is to be spent, to which the Commission has to respond. It also looks at the Court of Auditor's report, and how Community institutions have responded to its audit. The Council has retained control of what is known as 'compulsory' expenditure (basically the CAP with a few relics from the ECSC), but has a say over 'non-compulsory' expenditure, which it can increase or decrease within the limits set down by Maastricht. Article 209a binds Member States to taking the same measures to fight fraud against the Community as they would against fraud internally, and to co-ordinate their actions through liaison between the relevant bodies.

The procedure for international negotiations was altered in Article 228, with the European Parliament being consulted, apart from agreements concerning the common commercial policy, which effectively is to do with common tariffs (Article 113.3), where the Council is still the ultimate arbiter. 228a is a new article to cover the common foreign and security policy, adopted by the Treaty on European Union.

NEW AREAS OF CO-OPERATION INTRODUCED BY THE TREATY ON EUROPEAN UNION

Foreign and security policy

The Maastricht Treaty declared that it 'established' a common foreign and security policy. The Single European Act laid down that Member States should strive towards consistency and an outward-looking common policy. This was now to be formalised rather than just recommended, and the goals of these common policies were defined (Article J.1.2):

— to safeguard the common values, fundamental interests and independence of the Union;

— to strengthen the security of the Union and its Member States in all ways;

— to preserve peace and strengthen international security, in accordance with the principles of the United Nations Charter as well as the principles of the Helsinki Final Act and the objectives of the Paris Charter;

— to promote international co-operation;

— to develop and consolidate democracy and the rule of law, and respect for human rights and fundamental freedoms.

Article J.1.4 continues:

The Member States shall support the Union's external and security policy actively and unreservedly in a spirit of loyalty and mutual solidarity. They shall refrain from any action which is contrary to the interests of the Union or likely to impair its effectiveness as a cohesive force in international relations. The Council shall ensure that these principles are complied with.

It was also laid down that eventually a common defence policy would follow, with common defence forces a possibility. Some initiatives have been taken in this respect already, notably the co-operation between France and Germany in the formation of a single multinational force. This force may expand, but issues of command and territorial operability could reduce its effectiveness. (It was only recently that the Germans voted to allow their forces abroad, and the initial deployment has only been of transport aircraft to assist the United Nations in former Yugoslavia.)

Because foreign policy is conducted at a government level, it is left to the Council to determine what common action will be, how long it will go on for, and how it will be put into effect. The President of the Council, with the assistance of the previous and subsequent Presidents, represents the EU. Common action is to be decided by qualified majority and Member States are expected to abide by it. The Council decides whether common action is necessary according to guidelines set by the European Council; it has to agree unanimously, except where *it* makes provision for a qualified majority on decisions. All issues which entail military involvement have to be unanimous. Member States and the Commission can also submit proposals to the Council, and put questions to it on the common foreign policy. If Member States want to take independent national action on a relevant issue, they must inform the Council for consultations if time permits. The European Parliament is to be consulted on the broad outlines of foreign policy by the President and can query the Council's decisions and make recommendations to it. The Treaty specifies that the EP should hold an annual debate on progress in the common foreign and security policy.

The Western European Union (WEU), a semi-dormant international organisation, was revived on defence issues. In the declarations attached to the Maastricht Treaty the WEU was specified as the vehicle for European joint action (Declaration 30):

1. WEU Member States agree on the need to develop a genuine European security and defence identity and a greater European responsibility on defence matters ... WEU will form an integral part of the process of the development of the European Union and will enhance its contribution to solidarity within the Atlantic Alliance. WEU Member States agree to strengthen the role of WEU, in the longer-term perspective of a common defence, compatible with that of the Atlantic Alliance [NATO].

2. WEU will be developed as the defence component of the European Union and as a means to strengthen the European pillar of the Atlantic Alliance. To this end, it will formulate common European defence policy and carry forward its concrete implementation through the further development of its own operational role.

Its revival was primarily due to the fact that it fell outside other treaty organisations, such as NATO, which have a transatlantic component. With the development of a common defence policy, a vehicle would have to have been created if it did not already exist to carry out the detailed planning. Not all EU countries are members of the WEU; Ireland, Greece and Denmark still have to join, and Denmark negotiated an opt-out from the common defence policy. Participation in the WEU does not prevent Member States from observing their obligations under NATO or from co-ordinating joint actions, so long as these do not conflict with Maastricht provisions. There is a problem with the revival of the WEU in that non-EU members have been invited to join the WEU, and it is difficult to see how they would fit with a common defence policy – particularly Turkey, given its relations with Greece – but then exclusion, particularly in this case, would have unknown political ramifications.

Member States are also expected to keep other Member States (which do not participate in international organisations of which they are part) fully informed of the deliberations of those organisations, as are Member States which belong to the UN Security Council (currently the United Kingdom and France). Security Council members are also expected to defend the position of the EU in that forum.

A 'Political Committee' was also instituted to 'monitor the international situation in the areas covered by common foreign and security policy' and to advise the Council on policy.

The administrative budget is charged to the European Communities' budget. The executive budget for the implementation of the common policy can be charged to the Commission, where the Council unanimously agrees, or charged to the Member States, for which a scale of contributions is to be decided.

Development of the common foreign policy

This second pillar of Maastricht, the common foreign policy, has so far proved dismally ineffective. When the civil war in ex-Yugoslavia erupted, the EU was able to appoint a peacemaking envoy, Dr David Owen, who began working with his American counterpart Cyrus Vance. There are those who suggest that Dr Owen's record with the Labour Party – off which he formed a splinter group, the Social Democratic Party, which then allied with the Liberal Party before breaking off again – did not ideally qualify him for the role of peacemaker. But that is to miss the point. When European troops were sent – the French and British providing the largest contingents – it was under the auspices of the UN, not the EU. Even though Yugoslavia is physically within EU borders – Austria and Italy to the north and west, Greece to the south – the Member States demonstrated insufficient political will to act in unison. Germany bounced the EU into recognising Croatia by unilaterally doing so; similarly Chancellor Kohl has promised Poland that it will be a Member State by 2000, essentially to placate the Polish over some bilateral friction. Greece has proved intransigent in its refusal to allow the EU to recognise Macedonia under that name, and it is in theory the Republic of Skopje. Given that the ancient Greeks considered the Macedonians barbarians and the Macedonians did not regard themselves as Greeks, this is a little surprising, but the name of Alexander the Great still resonates and the Greeks would like to claim him for themselves. The delay caused in recognition was seen as particularly unhelpful in that recognition per se was perceived as the way of ensuring that Macedonia was not dragged into the civil war.

There is no doubt, though, that the EU feels a duty to develop an international political voice that matches its economic importance as the largest market in the world (by value). In that sense it is analogous to Germany, which has long been the dominant economic power, without having proportionate military importance; 1995 was a watershed though for German external involvement, as the Bundestag authorised the use of Luftwaffe transport aircraft to assist the UN in ex-Yugoslavia. This reversal of earlier restraint by Germany perhaps makes an EU common defence policy more likely, as without Germany it would have been somewhat hollow. France, however, despite the formation of a joint force with Germany, still has a tendency to act unilaterally, as was most recently demonstrated by the nuclear tests at Mururoa atoll. In the face of worldwide condemnation – including the barracking of President Chirac by MEPs at his post-electoral address of the European Parliament – France still went ahead. This sort of action will have to stop if the EU is to have a genuine common policy; Member States recognise this, but are exceedingly jealous of their sovereign powers in this field, while also being aware that unilateral individual action is becoming an increasingly unrealistic option where international crises need solution (the Gulf War, for example). Interestingly, the Commission is to send EU monitors to Mururoa at the time of writing to determine whether the tests infringe EAEC rules concerning dangerous nuclear testing.

Co-operation in the fields of justice and home affairs

The European Community has become something of a magnet to outsiders, both from Eastern Europe after the collapse of Communism, and to the inhabitants of the Mediterranean basin, particularly the ex-French colonies on the North African coast. With the greater freedom of movement that has characterised the development of the European Community, it was felt that internal co-operation should be increased. Terrorism, the drugs trade and immigration are important concerns for EU countries, and they felt it necessary to respond by co-ordinating various policies – essentially tightening external borders and more cohesive internal policing – so as to prevent abuse of the new freedoms.

Article K.1 of the Maastricht Treaty sets out the areas of common interest:

1. Asylum policy;

2. Rules for the external borders of the EU;
3. Immigration policy
   (a) conditions for entry and movement for third-country nationals;
   (b) residence conditions, including reunion of families and employment;
   (c) keeping out unauthorised immigrants.

4. 'Combating drug addiction';

5. 'Combating fraud on an international scale';

6. 'Judicial co-operation in civil matters';

7. 'Judicial co-operation in criminal matters';

8. 'Customs co-operation';

9. Police co-operation against terrorism, the drug trade, international crime in general, where relevant in co-operation with customs and the formation of 'a Union-wide system for exchanging information within a European Police Office (Europol).

In Article K.2 the Community agrees to abide by the European Convention for the Protection of Human Rights and Fundamental Freedoms of 1950, and the Convention relating to the Status of Refugees of 1951. Asylum would continue to be granted to people escaping political persecution.

Asylum policy has generally been that those who are politically persecuted at home have the right to asylum on reaching a 'safe' country. There have been arguments between EU nations over granting asylum: the United Kingdom has held that if an asylum seeker has landed first in another EU country before reaching Britain, then that is where he or she should seek asylum. Because of the apparently ever-increasing number of asylum seekers from all parts of the world, many of whom it is felt are economic migrants, a distinction is now drawn between the types of asylum seekers. Now it is not enough to have fled a repressive regime or a civil war; it is also necessary to show that you, the asylum seeker, were under some personal threat from that regime or the combatants. The Treaty also lays down that asylum policy should be harmonised.

Concerns over immigration have grown over the last few years. Germany in particular has had a vast influx, primarily from Central and Eastern Europe, with the flow increasing during the civil war in ex-Yugoslavia. It already has a large Turkish immigrant population. France has a large established immigrant population from Algeria and Tunisia; recently, fears of spillovers from the war between fundamentalists and the Algerian government (after the latter lost the election in 1992 but refused to step down) have been made more real by the Paris Métro bombs, and Le Pen's National Front has made some gains in the 1995 mayoral elections, especially in the south of France where fear of immigrants is more intense. Italy has seen waves of Albanian immigrants over the last few years as well, following the collapse of the Hoxha regime. The United Kingdom did not offer Hong Kong Chinese full British passports, so an influx is not expected from this source in 1997; whereas the Portuguese have offered residents of Macao – also to be reintegrated into China – national passports, and under EU law any Macao citizens who take up the offer will have full working and residence rights throughout the EU.

A Co-ordinating Committee was set up to assist the Council and the Commission in carrying out work in these areas, and the Presidency and the Commission are supposed to keep the European Parliament up to date on developments. The European Parliament is also supposed to hold an annual debate on progress.

The European Economic Area

In preparation for the possible accession of other European states, the Agreement on the European Economic Area was signed in 1992, which extended many free-trade rights to the EFTA countries. Austria, Sweden and Finland are now members of the EU, leaving only Switzerland and Norway outside the Union, and Switzerland outside the EEA.

THE SOCIAL CHAPTER

Originally, the Maastricht Treaty was to have included a social dimension building on the social policy that has been spelt out in earlier treaties. But the United Kingdom, under Margaret Thatcher's leadership and then with John Major's hand on the pen, refused to sign a treaty containing such provisions, fearing 'socialism by the back door', so the social policy was moved into a separate protocol which the other eleven members signed. Technically, it is known as the 'Community Charter of Fundamental Social Rights for Workers'.

Reading it though, it seems to state nothing exceptionable. Article 1 states the following:

> The Community and the Member States shall have as their objectives the promotion of employment, improved living and working conditions, proper social protection, dialogue between management and labour, the development of

human resources with a view to high lasting employment and the combating of exclusion. To this end, the Community and Member States shall implement measures which take account of the diverse forms of national practices, in particular in the field of contractual relations, and the need to maintain the competiveness of the Community economy.

This agenda would seem perfectly reasonable; true, Article 2 refers specifically to 'the information and consultation of workers' and to 'equality between men and women with regard to labour market opportunities and treatment at work'. Article 2 also allows the Council to set minimum conditions for the workplace, by qualified majority. The United Kingdom, though, as represented by the Tory government, fears better employee representation in industry – the idea of workers' representatives sitting on the board, as in Germany, is anathema to them – and also does not have a particularly good record on equal pay for equal work as set out in Article 119 of the Treaty of Rome. The aim of the social charter is to combine protection for workers with competition – to have a level playing field for competition, but at a higher level. Free-market thinkers, though, would like to 'price' labour back into the market; in practice this means that employers have to offer the bare minimum to attract the unemployed, with no reference to whether pay is a living wage, whatever the number of hours worked. Minimum wages are a vexed subject, but there is some evidence to show that in fact they create stability if set at the right level. Too high, and they will reduce employment; too low, and they will not attract the unemployed. And freeing up a labour market is not that effective when the entire structure of people's working lives is being changed, as is happening now. Those made 'free' from 'sunset' industries are rarely suitable for employment in 'sunrise' industries because of reasons of age, education and geographical and linguistic mobility. The old heavy industries and those of mass production where efficiency was achieved through the 'routinisation' of work are declining, or being forced out of business by developing countries where wages are significantly lower. Thus Japan took over much world ship-building, before it was taken over in turn by Korea as Japanese wealth and wages rose. The Japanese assault on the European and American car industries has been followed by the Koreans and Malaysians. White-collar jobs are under threat from computerisation – much clerical work having disappeared in banks and elsewhere – and middle management too is finding itself redundant. Trying to compete with developing countries on a wage basis in basic industries can only mean the impoverishment of workers, i.e. taking their wage levels down to those prevailing in Malaya, say, or India. The route that the Commission prefers is that of ensuring that Europe establishes itself in the industries of the future; for many this is a frightening proposition, but the automation of many of the unpleasant or boring chores of work by welding robots or automatic checkouts (to take two extreme examples) not only leads to an increase in efficiency but also liberates those involved. Agreed, re-education is necessary – and the Community places a great deal of emphasis on vocational training – but not to have to work in factories or in the vast clerical halls of the past has to be an improvement. But the period of structural change is painful for those involved, especially as it can last a long time (some commentators regard the 'information revolution', during which information services overtook manufacturing in value, as having started over fifty years ago).

The irony for the United Kingdom ultimately is that companies which operate according to EU rules outside Britain will find it difficult not to accord their British workers the same rights. The number of companies in this position is increasing, so the United Kingdom may well end up being in the position where it effectively abides by an agreement in which it has no say, as the opt-out specifically excludes Britain from voting in the Council on these issues. Trades unions are also forming EU-wide groupings (e.g. the ETUC, the European Trades Unions Congress), which make it harder and more pointless for a state to opt out. Also the perceived 'threat' of Scandinavian or French or German levels of worker protection was always going to be reduced by the ability of the poorer EU countries to pay for them. The United Kingdom would have had allies within the Council in any event.

CHAPTER 7

The Future

The next important event in the chronology of the EU is the 1996 Intergovernmental Conference, at which issues such as the expansion of the Union and progress on the Maastricht Treaty, especially the provisions regarding monetary union – the single currency – will be discussed. The original deadline of 1 January 1997 for monetary union looks increasingly unlikely even for the 'core' group (the Benelux countries, Germany and France) and even 1 January 1999 may be too optimistic. The debate about a single currency is growing more heated as its deadline approaches; Bernard Connolly, a British economist working at the Commission, wrote that EMU would eventually lead to war between France and Germany. This is rather an extreme prognosis, but more voices are raised shifting the argument from 'when' to 'if'. In 1995 the Governor of the Bank of England, Eddie George, declared that a single currency would lead to widespread unemployment in the hard-currency countries, as jobs fled to soft-currency countries (just as they have done in NAFTA – the North American Free Trade Area – from the United States to Mexico). There is no doubt that the deflationary *franc-fort* policy has led France to much agony, with very high unemployment, disguised through vocational and other schemes, and real deprivation. Areas that relied heavily on tourism, including many rural parts, are really feeling the pinch, as tourists simply stay away or, if they do come, spend as little as possible. Youth unemployment, defined as unemployment for those under 25, is particularly severe, being around 25 per cent over much of the country apart from the Ile de France (Paris) and Alsace. Figures this high, especially where the unemployed remain unemployed for a long period (some of them will probably *never* work) are a recipe for major social upheaval, especially as the social security net comes under increasing strain – fewer contributors and more claimants.

The convergence criteria for a single currency look increasingly unlikely to be met. Germany, France, Luxembourg and the United Kingdom will almost certainly meet them (though even mighty Germany's public debt has temporarily exceeded the criterion due to the strain of reunification), but Belgium and Italy have public debts that exceed their GDP and thus will take years to bring down to the required level. However, it would be very odd if Belgium, essentially at the heart of the EU and one of the few places where a substantial body of people think in ECUs, were not part of EMU. But if it is to be part of EMU then the rules will have to be changed, which will not appeal to the financially prudent Germans who are worried enough about dilution of their currency. While the ECU may seem stable enough to weak-currency countries, partly because swings in one currency compensate for swings in another, to the Germans it is hardly preferable to the mark. Furthermore the United Kingdom, despite its probable eligibility, is showing every sign of not wanting to join EMU, though this may change after the next General Election, which will occur at the latest in April 1997. Indeed some heads of government – Helmut Kohl, for example – have made no bones about the fact that they are quite happy to stall the decision-making process on some issues until after this election, when it is presumed a more Europhile Labour government will be in power. Italy conversely would dearly like to join EMU, and so we are left with the situation where two of the larger EU Member States cannot or will not participate.

Jacques Santer has expressed his determination that a single currency will be in place: 'EMU [European Monetary Union] is not a pipedream and it is becoming more concrete as time moves on. I ask you, is it any good if the margins on trade and investment

Member State budget deficits and cumulative national debt

	Government borrowing (GDP %)	Cumulative national debt (GDP %)
Belgium	4.3	139.3
Denmark	2.1	77.6
Germany	2.4	58.4
Greece	9.0	112.3
Spain	5.9	64.5
France	5.1	53.5
Ireland	2.2	86.1
Italy	7.4	116.4
Luxembourg	1.1	7.6
Netherlands	3.3	80.3
Austria	4.6	65.9
Portugal	5.2	70.4
Finland	4.5	66.3
Sweden	9.0	84.2
United Kingdom	4.9	52.5

flows can be wiped out by the vagaries of exchange-rate markets in a matter of days?'

The debate about currency union intertwines with another debate, that of a two (or more) speed Europe, with phrases such as 'variable geometry' (particularly beloved of British politicians, though what aircraft wings have to do with politics is hard to fathom) or 'Europe à la carte'. Increasingly the Franco-German-Benelux axes are seen as forming a core Europe, consisting of devout Unionists, co-operating closely with each other whilst leaving the other countries to fend for themselves at the margin. The geographically peripheral Member States, the Iberian countries, Ireland and Greece (the newly Unionised Scandinavian states are seen as economically close to the core) are unhappy at such talk, partly because they are net beneficiaries of the EU and partly because they see the EU as the road whereby they can reach a similar economic status to the core countries.

For several years now there has been a debate between those

who want to 'broaden' the Union and those who want to 'deepen' it. The United Kingdom is the leading proponent of the broadening team which wants to see the EU as an economic union, i.e. a fully functioning single market. They wish to broaden it – that is, let in many more countries – because they believe that by doing so political integration will become harder to achieve. The French and the Germans are of the 'deepening' school, believing we should consolidate the economic and political progress made so far (*pace* Chancellor Kohl's promise to Poland). The French in particular are worried because of the fall of the Communist regimes in Eastern Europe and the reunification of Germany, because they fear that Bonn (soon to be Berlin) will shift its focus to the East. For them, deepening the bond with Germany is still a priority.

There are also other major issues involved in inviting more states into the Union. The CAP has not yet been fully reformed (it still consumes just under 50 per cent of the EU budget) and adding Member States whose economies still have large agricultural sectors would place an intolerable burden on it and thereby the net contributor countries (Germany, the United Kingdom, Sweden and Austria). The keenest 'broadener', the United Kingdom, thus faces a conundrum – less political integration perhaps, but higher contributions.

Broadening the Community will also bring further difficulties; even with 12 Member States the EU had nine official languages, to which Finnish (which is totally unrelated to any other European language) and Swedish have now had to be added.

THE 1996 INTERGOVERNMENTAL CONFERENCE (IGC)

The Treaty of Maastricht set out a timetable for reviewing progress on its two main innovations, the common foreign policy and the common justice and home affairs policy, and this process will take place at Corfu. IGCs were few and far between in the early days of the European Union; there was one in 1950–51 to set up the ECSC, and another over 1955–57 to set up the EEC and the EAEC. Since 1985 there have been three – one in 1985 itself which led to the Single European Act and two in 1990–91 which led to the

Treaty of Maastricht. The increasing number of IGCs reflects the accelerating pace of EU activity over the years, partly due to the dynamic leadership of Jacques Delors who was determined to restore momentum to the process of European unification which, partly due to recession, had faltered.

When Maastricht was signed the signatories were fully aware that because of the changes in Europe – the fall of the Berlin Wall, the collapse of Communism in Central and Eastern Europe and in the Soviet Union itself – geopolitics had become very fluid, and would remain so for several years. The fledgling democracies to the east would take time to become politically stable and their economies would take several years to unravel the legacy of Communism. As we know, the Russian (Commonwealth of Independent States) economy recorded several years of contraction, as did those of its near neighbours; both ex-Soviet states such as Ukraine and ex-Communist states such as Hungary and democratic Finland were badly hit by the loss of what had been a major export market. One of the consequences of the Russian implosion was that middle European states had to shift their whole economic focus from looking eastward to looking west.

The main issues which the Maastricht Treaty made provision for assessing and revising were:

— subsidiarity – taking decision-making down as close as possible to the citizen
— balanced social and economic progress in the internal market
— the common foreign and security policy
— protection of citizens' rights
— co-operation in justice and home affairs
— the sharing of legislative powers between the Council and the European Parliament
— extension of EU competence into the fields of energy, civil protection and tourism

Preparations are under way: because of the complexity of the issues to be addressed, a Reflection Group was set up consisting of one representative of each Member State's foreign ministry,

Commissioner Marcelino Oreja, and two MEPs. The Group began work in June 1995, and will submit its final report to the European Council meeting in Madrid in December. The June European Council was devoted to the IGC agenda, and a special European Council has been called by the Spanish President to review the Group's progress. In January IGC negotiations are scheduled to commence.

Declarations by the European Council and the Council indicated that there is a priority list of items for the IGC, much of which are concerned with the mechanics of legislation. It is felt that the current decision-making process is too complex and should be simplified. There is also the question as to whether the qualified majority rules should be changed so that more issues are covered, and whether the weightings of votes should more closely reflect population size. With expansion of the Council with the accession of new members, unanimity will completely block the decision-making process. Jacques Santer in his first speech in the United Kingdom put it quite clearly:

> We cannot enlarge the EU without significant policy changes and some institutional reform ... There must be only a very few areas where a qualified majority vote does not apply, or enlargement means a monkey wrench jammed into our institutional machinery.
>
> It is simply not acceptable because of institutional bickering and in-fighting that we are too often paralysed in taking any action ... No Member State can just expect to make hay in its favourite areas and block everyone else in theirs because that leads to political gridlock. Worse still, blocking in specific areas will mean the chances of achieving one's own priorities may be much reduced. A policy of give and take is required.

The Commission now has 20 members already, and expansion of the Union to 25 members would lead to 38, at which point it will become almost unmanageable. Jacques Delors has recommended that its size be reduced, which would mean that all Member States had one Commissioner.

Strengthening of the powers of the European Parliament to increase its powers of co-decision would help reduce the democratic deficit, and the Parliament itself, like all parliaments through history, would like to increase its powers. With the prospective expansion of the Union, the issue of numbers also arises – should these be reduced? Currently there are 626 MEPs, so many that MEPs often find they have little opportunity to speak in debates, and enlargement of the EU can only make this worse. Some commentators have suggested that a lower house should have no more than about 350 members. Implicit in this is the suggestion of an upper house rather on the lines of the US Congress, with the European Parliament becoming a population-based House of Representatives and a new body becoming the Senate. The proposal for an upper house comes from the French, and from Leo Tindemans (ex-Belgian Prime Minister and an MEP) who have suggested that it be composed of representatives from Member State parliaments, thus greatly strengthening the link between them and national parliaments. They have also suggested that all Member States should have a minister for EU affairs. Tindemans has stated that his bicameral European Parliament should have equal status to the Council – 'Parliament would represent European citizens and the Council the Member States'. The two Councils are also aware that procedures need simplifying for justice and home affairs. Finally, the European Parliament is actively drafting a proper European Constitution, though whether this would ever be accepted is a different matter.

Common foreign and security policy are seen as having made little progress since Maastricht, a failure attributed to a lack of political will. The priorities of Member States differ markedly for historical and geographical reasons – for example, one would expect Greece and Denmark to have common views on only the most general of issues. Defence is tied in with this, though there is pressure to act in that the WEU treaty is due for renewal in 1998, and a decision will need to be made as to whether the WEU should become the formal defence organ of the EU. The end of the Cold War, and the long-proclaimed desire of the United States to hand over responsibility for European defence entirely to the Europeans (the USA still has 100,000 troops in Europe), make it more pressing that the EU set up a proper defence organisation. There are problems in that some Member States – Sweden, Denmark, Finland and Ireland – adhere firmly to a neutrality policy. Also, whatever structure is set up has to respect the sensitivities of the EU's eastern neighbours, especially if expansion includes former Warsaw Pact countries (not to mention the Baltic states, Lithuania, Latvia and Estonia, which are eager to join). President Yeltsin has rumbled frequently about a revival of the Cold War, and more extremist, populist politicians such as Zhirinovsky express open hostility to the West, including Europe. Partly their pronouncements are due to disappointment with the amount of assistance Russia has received from Europe (one of the weak points of the common European foreign policy was the EU's less than open-handedness – no Marshall Plan for Russia – but this was due in no small part to Germany's absorption in restructuring the East German economy, and the costs attributable thereto), and partly due to traditional fears. Invasions of Russia come from the east or the west (not the south), and foreign troops who have trod its soil this century, and not as allies, include the Poles, British, French, Americans, Rumanians, Hungarians, Spanish, Finns, Austrians, Italians and, of course, the Germans.

Jacques Santer has focused on a variety of issues for the first year of his Presidency. He views the progress on the 1992 reforms as having been in general successful, but seems to have a great concern for the ordinary citizen.

All too often, the public are left feeling that the single market was purely business-oriented. They do not understand why there are still identity checks at borders within the Union. After reading the Treaty and what it says in Article 7a, I wonder why people are still having to wait in long queues at airports.

Then there is the endless bureaucratic nonsense that sometimes makes moving from one Member State to another a real obstacle course. It continues to amaze me that something as ordinary as a driving licence is not always recognised automatically anywhere in the Union without further ado. I would like to see a bit more common sense and more room for mutual recognition. I feel that our authorities should make more of an effort to put themselves in the public's shoes ... [not] making life difficult for ordinary people with all this red tape.

Santer wants the activities of the EU to have meaning for the private citizen and for its processes to be clear:

The European citizen does not want to know all the ins and outs of everything, but he does want to know who is doing what, who to blame and who to praise for this decision or that piece of legislation that concerns him.

Santer is often seen as a consolidator rather than an innovator, such as Delors, and the details of his 1995 programme bore this out. He expressed a determination both to make sure that EU rules for the internal market are properly implemented and observed, with the Commission in its watchdog role, and to fill in the gaps in legislation. For example, one proposal re the right of residence specifies that current legislation should be 'recast' to incorporate the decisions of the Court of Justice. Other items specifically listed are a finalised system for VAT and harmonisation of excise duties and a carbon tax – i.e. items which have been on the agenda for a long time, but discussed rather than dealt with. Santer has stated that it is critical to tighten up and simplify as much of the existing legislation as possible before the accession of new Member States. He has also specified that they will have to abide by the *acquis Communitaire* – the shorthand term for all EU legislation and decisions taken by the date of their accession. When a new state joins it is presumed to be at the same stage as the pre-existing members, and has to make the legislative adjustments necessary.

CHAPTER 8

Epilogue

While we think mostly in terms of free markets and economic development when we think of the EU, it should never be forgotten that social and political developments were esteemed equally important by its founding fathers. The route to prosperity was the route to peace. And maintaining peace is not a static process – the institutions of peace need to be constantly active, in the spirit more than the letter of the agreements from which they were born; left to themselves, human institutions disintegrate. There must be constant dynamism to ensure that a sense of purpose is never absent, and that original visions translate into concrete action. Vigilance is necessary to ensure that all shoulders are put to the common wheel of progress. Forces for centripetalism and forces for centrifugalism are in constant tension, and need to be managed with skill and diplomacy, so that where organisation is needed organisation exists, and where private freedoms do not conflict they are encouraged to flourish.

The EU is by no means perfect. It is only human nature for people to see most clearly their immediate local interests without understanding how they will be improved by broader, long-term action. Persuading peoples of the ultimate benefits is a slow process. The EU still has a long road down which to travel to establish the most effective institutions, and they too will have to change as the world changes. With our daily newspapers and our hourly newsflashes we expect change to be instantaneous, and are constantly frustrated by its apparent slowness and with the difficulties encountered. But it should not be forgotten that the United States had to tread a long slow path to become a true nation, via a horrible civil war 80 years after its foundation.

The true question is whether it is better than the alternatives that might exist – a peaceful Europe, maybe, but one that is fragmented, too small to compete effectively with its world competitors, a set of nations condemning themselves to an economic and political backwater.

In Mark Twain's *The Mysterious Stranger* his spokesman for common sense, Satan's nephew (also named Satan but not a devil) states:

> Monarchies, aristocracies, and religions [to which we would add repressive regimes and nationalism in the sense of jingoistic patriotism – Dr Johnson's 'last refuge of the scoundrel'] are all based on that large defect in your race – the individual's distrust of his neighbor, and his desire, for safety's or comfort's sake, to stand well in his neighbor's eye...
>
> ... The loud little handful – as usual – will shout for the war. The pulpit will – warily and cautiously – object – at first; the great, big, dull bulk of the nation will rub its sleepy eyes and try to make out why there should be a war and will say, earnestly and indignantly, 'It is unjust and dishonorable and there is no necessity for it.' Then the handful will shout louder. A few fair men on the other side will argue and reason against the war with speech and pen, and at first will have a hearing and be applauded, but it will not last long; those others will outshout them, and presently the anti-war audiences will thin out and lose popularity. Before long you will see this curious thing: the speakers stoned from the platform, and free speech strangled by hordes of furious men who in their secret hearts are still at one with those stoned speakers – as earlier – but do not dare to say so ... Next the statesmen will invent cheap lies ... and every man will be glad of those conscience-smoothing falsities ... and will

thank God for the better sleep he enjoys after this process of grotesque self-deception.

As a prediction of what has happened in much of Europe this century, Twain's could hardly be bettered. The remedies against it are also obvious: governments that are as open and democratic as possible, and the forging of political, social and economic links that bind people across Europe, utterly transcending the old hard exclusive borders of nationalism.

CHAPTER 9

Euromyths –
the Distorting Prism

One unexpected by-product of the EU's legislative programme, which initially seemed harmless and laughable but which now causes the Commission some concern – because it projects such an unreal Kafka-esque image of the EU – is the Euromyth. These are particularly prevalent in the British press, which clearly generally reads neither published EU legislation nor itself, in that some stories appear as regularly as Augusts, sometimes in the same paper. Whether a sinister construction should be put on these stories is another matter. As fiction or distorted information they can have a propagandistic effect, and the editorial policy of some British papers has definitely been anti-EU. However, governments are not above using the EU or the Commission as a whipping-boy, as when the Department of National Heritage stated that public money could not be given to charitable projects which were already receiving cash from the National Lottery, blaming this clearly unpopular rule on a non-existent EU regulation. Naturally and rightly, 'Brussels' complained. The Swedes may be getting in on the act too, with strawberry producers in that country up in arms at the fact that their etiolated northern fruit does not qualify as a Euro-strawberry as it is not over 25mm in diameter, with 35mm being the grade one size. Or so it has been reported in the Swedish press which has in some respects followed the British example, in that it finds it easier to blame problems such as declining currency and unemployment on the EU – which it has so recently joined – than on its own government's policies.

Many Euromyths derive from the fact that anything with 'Europe' in the title is somehow deemed to be due to the EU (*viz.* below the Christmas Tree Growers Association of Western Europe). Also, because journalists are expected to write stories they often choose 'handles', frequently factitious threats to revered products or traditional methods – as with Scotch whisky distilleries being banned from keeping their earth floors; they were not, but there is an EU directive which requires that floors, including earth ones, be clean on sites used for products for human consumption. And there is much misunderstanding of standards – for example 'small' apples have a minimum diameter of 50mm, 'large' of 65mm. The purpose of this standard is to ensure that fruit is sufficiently large to have had the chance to ripen, so that the consumer can be confident that it is ready to eat by the time it is in the shop. Other standards are requested by the producing bodies simply so that everybody knows when they see the classification of a product what size, shape, etc. it conforms to. It is not illegal to grow bent cucumbers, for example, but a packer naturally likes to know beforehand how many fit into a box. Many standards derive from world standards, simply being adopted in EU legislation. The whole thing can be put in perspective if one recognises that essentially standards have three roles: they provide levels of classification, as for natural products; they guarantee the interoperability of manufactured or processed products; and they inform the consumer that a product is safe. The first type of standard is not mandatory, it is classificatory – i.e. if an apple is over a certain diameter it is defined as 'large', but this does not mean that 'medium' or 'small' apples are banned or that such a thing as the Euro-apple exists! We don't even think about the fact that petrol is the same; whether we are in France or the United Kingdom or Germany, for example, we simply assume that it has been refined to common standards, which it has, and here again it is the refiners and the car manufacturers who have called for the standards. As for safety standards, nobody can object to these being as high as possible, and all governments have their own health and safety legislation which the EU is trying to co-ordinate to a common high standard.

Currently the Commission has 130 British Euromyths on its lists, presumably so few because it is impossible to keep up with the constant flow. They need refuting and misunderstandings need to be explained.

They fall into three categories: outright nonsense, nonsensical constructions based on one or two half-digested facts, and simple misunderstandings of the meaning of EU pronouncements. This is strange as much of what the EU produces – precisely because it has to be translated into so many languages – is very clear.

OUTRIGHT NONSENSE

A Directive makes hairnets obligatory for fishermen when on board their boats.
... clearly a sinister threat to the masculinity and self-esteem of fishermen ...

This derives from a Council Directive laying down that strict hygiene should be observed in *fish-processing*, both at the dockside and elsewhere. Suitable headgear should be worn to prevent hair contaminating processed fish, just as it is in other food preparation, according to widespread hygiene regulations. Of course, if fishermen are wearing their sou'westers they would probably meet these requirements, even though they don't need to.

The EU ordered Grimsby to stop smelling of fish.
... Brussels believes it can assume the mantle of the Deity, and achieve the impossible ...

There is no EU legislation requiring smells to be kept within certain bounds. However, there is the United Kingdom's 1990 Environmental Protection Act which aims to control air pollution. Local authorities are responsible for issuing licences and enforcing them.

The last producer of Caerphilly cheese in Caerphilly is to be forced out of business having been told it is illegal to transport unpasteurised milk in metal churns.

... a typical EU-Goliath versus plucky little David 'real' food producer, as obsessive bureaucrats cast their net ever wider, in their desire to winkle out any deviation from a sanitised bland Euro-product ...

What the Council's directives actually say is that containers for UHT and pasteurised milk of over four litres should be hermetically sealed during transport. The provisions do not cover raw milk, though in fact it is normal practice to transport it in sealed containers. On balance, it would seem more hygienic for any milk not to be exposed to the elements during transport. It was reported that the producer would have to lay a 75ft-pipeline to transport milk, but this was simply untrue.

Euro-Christmas trees must be symmetrical, with regularly spaced needles, have the same roots and be of the same colour.
... nature must bend to the will of the Commission, in the interests of complete Euro-conformity ...

The EU has promulgated no regulations at all about Christmas trees. There is however a Christmas Tree Growers Association of Western Europe which has drawn up specifications for Christmas trees, whose French and Danish members put forward a ten-category classification for the trees.

HALF-BAKED STORIES

Brussels will ban soya milk as it is not sufficiently clearly labelled for consumers to distinguish it from cow's milk.
... a wicked attempt to deny infants allergic to mother's milk and vegans a product essential to their existence ...

A Council Regulation had listed a number of products that had no dairy connection (e.g. cream crackers, cream soda) and it listed products which could *continue* to use such names. The UK government wanted to keep soya milk on the list, but other Member States opposed this. But this does not mean that soya milk will be banned – it is simply up to the United Kingdom and soya milk manufacturers to come up with a new designation and a timetable for implementing it.

Valentine cards infringe EU employment law as being a form of sexual harassment and will lead to an avalanche of claims, for which employers might be liable unless Valentine cards are banned from the workplace.
... Christmas cards will be next, as the Commission works towards its long-term goal of suppressing all forms of harmless pleasure ...

This was an artfully placed story for Valentine's day. What actually exists is a Commission Recommendation of 27 November 1991 which states:

> It is recommended that Member States take action to promote awareness that conduct of a sexual nature, or other conduct based on sex affecting the dignity of women and men at work, including conduct of superiors and colleagues, is unacceptable if:
> (a) such conduct is unwanted, unreasonable and offensive to the recipient;
> (b) a person's rejection of, or submission to, such conduct on the part of employers or workers (including superiors or colleagues) is used explicitly or implicitly as a basis for a decision which affects that person's access to vocational training, access to employment, promotion, salary or any other employment decisions;
> (c) such conduct creates an intimidating, hostile or humiliating work environment for the recipient;
> and that such conduct may, in certain circumstances be contrary to the principle of equal treatment ...'

Recommendations are not binding, but in any event none of the above can be considered in the least objectionable in an orderly and well-run workplace. As clause (a) states, unwanted conduct (into which category a Valentine may or may not fall) which is offensive is unacceptable.

Paperboys and -girls to be banned by EU.
... and when taxes are finally harmonised, newsagents will be instructed by Brussels to deduct the basic rate of income tax ...

This is simply not true. The EC Directive stated that children in full-time education should be restricted to 15 hours per week and three hours per day. This work has to be done outside school hours and should take place between 6 in the morning and 8 at night, with some exceptions. No children should work between midnight and 4 in the morning.

The UK will be forced to abolish the zero-rate VAT on books.
... yet another attempt by Brussels to make one of life's basic pleasures more expensive ...

The truth is that zero-rated items can continue to be zero-rated until 1 January 1997, if the rate was applied before 1 January 1991. Therefore books can continue to be zero-rated until 1997.

Pubs will be forced to display price lists by the EU.
... if only ...

This is simply not true; this kind of legislation is left to individual governments. The Danes for example have decided that prices should be published. Some of us in the United Kingdom may remember that the government here did require prices to be published, i.e. visible to the consumer. As many readers who have been to a pub will have noticed, they are generally visible if one is (a) extremely long-sighted and (b) is very long-necked so as to be able to crane round pillars and other obstructions to use one's long sight. It is one of the few areas where consumers do not seem to insist on their rights, though presumably the importance of price declines in inverse proportion to the amount consumed.

THE WRONG END OF THE STICK

Engineering firms to be swamped in red tape due to Brussels' insistence that machines carry the 'CE' mark.
... red tape, like the evil mist in a science-fiction horror film, swirls around, spreading into every nook and cranny, asphyxiating those unfortunates whom it envelops ...

In fact manufacturers can choose which standards they wish to abide by; only 6 per cent of products require third-party certification, and then only if they were not made to a voluntary EU standard. In reality, if goods are made to the 'CE' standard or are certified, they avoid the need for testing in the EU's other 14 states. This actually represents a reduction in red tape and a cost saving.

Brussels blocking ban on 'bull' bars.
... mindless legislators show their indifference to the safety of ordinary citizens and children ...

Bull bars, the 'tough'-looking frameworks attached mostly to the fronts of 'designer' four-wheel-drive jeeps cruising the urban outback, are without doubt a danger to pedestrians and have increased the seriousness of injuries. There is already a Commission directive, which reflects national legislation, banning sharp edges and ornaments on vehicles, and the Commission is aware that the current situation is unsatisfactory, especially given the surprising growth in popularity of these vehicles. The current situation is set out below.

Member States can ban the registration of type-approved vehicles with bull bars originally fitted for six months on grounds of public safety, notifying the Commission and the exporting country of the reasons. During this period the country importing the vehicles and the exporting country can try to resolve their differences. After six months the ban lapses. Where EU type-approval has been given, such a ban technically infringes single market legislation.

Where a vehicle was type-approved without a bull bar, then any such bull bar can be banned, and where an original type-approved bull bar is replaced with a different one, this too can be banned. Where bull bars do not comply with the EU Directive on projections, simply having national type-approval, they can be banned under Article 36 (public safety).

The Commission is aware that the rules covering bull bars are unnecessarily complex, but the risk that they posed to pedestrians was not originally recognised, and steps will be taken to redress this.

An EU Directive to reduce money laundering has resulted in banks, building societies and the Post Office demanding ID, with a utility bill to prove one's address. How will children open accounts as they have never had to pay such bills?
... we have to do it already, but Brussels sticking its finger in naturally makes it a threat to children ...

Such a directive is in place, for when accounts are opened and when a transaction of over ECU 15,000 is made. But ID measures are up to national governments and, where appropriate, the industries themselves. The Directive was unanimously passed by the Council of Ministers, and followed a G7 (Group of Seven – leading industrial countries) recommendation which was approved unanimously. Much of the EU system is based on existing British rules. ID has long been required in the United Kingdom to set up an account, and children's accounts have been left to the discretion of the banks themselves. (After all, it is not beyond the wit of launderers and fraudsters to use children's accounts, and some precautions must be taken.)

EU standardisation leads to slow-boiling kettles due to voltage reduction.
... Euro-conformity threatens the cherished cup of tea ...

CENELEC has laid down a standard whereby all EU members will have to have a common voltage of 230 by the year 2003, down from the United Kingdom maximum of 240 (originally a band of 220–240). CENELEC is an independent committee supported by industry and not subsidised either by governments or the EU; it has 18 member countries including some outside the EU. The United Kingdom energy minister welcomed the decision as it means greater choice in the products one can buy. The Electricity Association in the United Kingdom confirmed that this reduction would not require any changes to existing equipment or cause any changes in its performance. It also noted that choice would be broadened, and that one of the benefits would be improved product safety.

Power limit to motorcycles of 100bhp interfering with the ordinary lives of citizens.

... Brussels threatens the cherished and ancient freedom of going at twice the speed limit rather than one and a half times ...

It is true that the EU has such a directive, but it was formulated on the advice of various road safety bodies. The argument that power leads to the ability to avoid accidents is fairly weak, given that speed limits apply over most of Europe and that in urban areas this is generally no more than 50kph or 30mph. Also the power-to-weight ratio of a powerful motorbike is massively more than that of a car. It is also argued that large motorbikes have fewer accidents than small ones; this is due to the fact that there are many fewer large expensive motorbikes and, of course, because of their initially high purchase price most are ridden by more experienced riders. Finally, all accidents on two wheels tend to be more serious than those on four. So the freedom to have more powerful motorbikes conflicts with the extra burden they place on society as a whole in insurance, medical costs etc. The arguments are similar to those that existed over wearing helmets.

Brief Chronology

1950	9 May	The Schuman Declaration proposing the ECSC for France and Germany.
1951	18 April	Treaty of Paris signed by the Six – France, Germany, Italy, the Netherlands, Belgium and Luxembourg.
1952	27 May	European Defence Community (EDC) Treaty signed in Paris – the first common European defence initiative.
1954	30 August	French Parliament rejects the EDC.
	23 October	Western European Union instituted.
1957	25 March	Treaties of Rome signed, EEC and EAEC come into being.
1958	1 January	Treaties of Rome come into force. The Commissions begin activity in Brussels.
1960	4 January	European Free Trade Association agreement signed in Stockholm.
1962	30 July	Introduction of the CAP.
1963	14 January	First of De Gaulle's 'Non, non et non' to British accession.
1965	8 April	The 'Merger' Treaty is signed, to come into force 1 January 1967.
1966	29 January	The 'Luxembourg' compromise. The French boycotted Council meetings because they did not agree with the principle of majority voting on many issues as laid down in the Treaty of Rome. It was agreed that despite the Treaty of Rome, decisions would not be made until

		unanimity had been reached, effectively establishing a veto. A major brake on Community progress.
1968	1 July	Final abolition of customs duties within the Community, and introduction of Common External Tariff.
1969	1–2 December	The Hague Summit agrees to formalise the CAP structure and the principle of 'own resources' (i.e. financial independence from Member States) for the Community.
1970	22 April	'Treaty amending Certain Budgetary Provisions' of the Rome Treaties and the Merger Treaty – prepares for introduction of 'own resources' and gives the European Parliament greater budgetary powers.
	30 June	Negotiations begin with Denmark, Ireland, Norway and the United Kingdom.
1972	23 January	Treaty signed for the accession of these four countries in Brussels.
	24 April	Currency 'snake' begins.
	25 September	Norwegian 'no' referendum kills application.
1974	9–10 December	Paris Summit agrees to heads of state or government meeting three times a year as the european Council and proposes direct elections to the EP and the setting up of the European Regional Development Fund.
1975	28 February	First Lomé Convention signed for aid programme to African, Caribbean and Pacific (ACP) states.
	22 July	'Treaty amending Certain Financial Provisions' of the Rome Treaties gives further budgetary powers to the EP and institutionalising the Court of Auditors is signed, as is the 'Treaty establishing a Single Council and a Single Commission of the European Communities', the 'Merger Treaty'.
1978	6–7 July	France and Germany present the European Monetary System to replace the 'snake' at Bremen European Council.
1979	13 March	EMS takes effect.
	28 May	Treaty on accession of Greece signed.

	7–10 July	First direct elections to EP.
	31 October	Second Lomé Convention signed.
1984	28 February	Esprit RTD programme adopted.
	14–17 June	Second direct elections to EP.
	25–26 June	Fontainebleau European Council agrees refunds to be granted to United Kingdom on its contribution to Community budget. (UK rebate agreed at 66 per cent of the excess of its VAT payments to the EC and the money spent in the UK by the EC.)
	8 December	Third Lomé Convention signed.
1985	12 March	Jacques Delors presents internal market programme to the European Parliament.
	14 June	Schengen Agreement signed between Benelux, France and Germany.
	2–4 December	Luxembourg European Council agrees to draw up Single European Act.
1986	1 January	Spain and Portugal join Community.
	17–18 February	Signing of Single European Act (SEA) in Luxembourg.
1987	14 April	Turkey applies for EC membership.
	1 July	SEA comes into force.
	26 October	WEU adopts common defence policy.
1988	25 June	Joint Declaration on establishing relations between EC and Comecon (the East European and Russian trade bloc).
1989	18 June	Third direct elections to the EP.
	17 July	Austria applies for EC membership.
	9 November	Collapse of Berlin Wall.
	9 December	European Council in Strasbourg agrees to convene Intergovernmental Conference (IGC).
	15 December	Fourth Lomé Convention signed.
1990	29 May	Agreement establishing the European Bank for Reconstruction and Development signed in Paris.
	19 June	Detailed Schengen Agreement conditions signed.
	4 July	Cyprus applies to join EC.
	16 July	Malta applies to join EC.
	3 October	Reunification of Germany.
	27 November	Italy joins Schengen states.

	14 December	Two IGCs begin in Rome to discuss economic and monetary union (EMU), and political union.
1991	1 July	Sweden applies to join EC.
	21 October	European Economic Area agreement signed between EC and EFTA.
	18 November	Spain and Portugal join Schengen states.
	9–10 December	Maastricht European Council.
1992	7 February	Maastricht Treaty is signed.
	18 March	Finland applies to join EC.
	22 May	Switzerland applies to join EC.
	2 June	Danish referendum rejects Maastricht.
	16 September	United Kingdom forced out of ERM by money markets.
	20 September	'Petit oui' in France – referendum approves Maastricht Treaty by 51.05 per cent.
1993	18 May	Second Danish referendum with renegotiated full opt-outs from monetary union secures 56.8 per cent majority in favour.
	12 July	United Kingdom Parliament ratifies Maastricht.
	12 October	German court ruling allows Maastricht to enter into force in Germany.
1994	1 January	Stage II of EMU begins. European Monetary Institute begins operating.
1995	1 January	Sweden, Austria and Finland enter EU.

APPENDIX 2

The Commission

PRESIDENT: Jacques Santer, Luxembourg
Responsibilites: Centralised EU functions and monetary matters with Yves-Thibault de Silguy, common foreign and security policy and human rights with Hans van den Broek.

VICE-PRESIDENT: Sir Leon Brittan, UK
Responsibilites: External relations with North America, Australia, New Zealand, China, Korea, Hong Kong, Macao and Taiwan. Common commercial policy, relations with the OECD and WTO.

VICE-PRESIDENT: Manual Marin, Spain
Responsibilities: External relations with southern Mediterranean countries, the Middle East, Latin America and Asia (apart from Sir Leon Brittan's responsibilities) including development aid.

Martin Bangemann, Germany
Industrial affairs, information and telecommunications technologies.

Karel van Miert, Belgium
Responsibilities: Competition.

Hans van den Broek, Holland
Responsibilities: External relations with Central and East European countries, former Soviet Union, Mongolia, Turkey, Cyprus, Malta and other European countries. Common foreign and security policy and human rights, with Jacques Santer.

João de Deus Pinheiro, Portugal
Responsibilites: External relations with African, Caribbean and Pacific (ACP) countries and South Africa, including development aid, and the Lomé Convention.

Marcelino Oreja, Spain
Responsibilites: Relations with the European Parliament and Member States (transparency, communication and information). Culture and audiovisual policy. Official publications. Institutional matters and preparations for the 1996 IGC.

Anita Gradin, Sweden
Responsibilites: Immigration, home affairs and justice.
Relations with the Ombudsman. Financial control. Fraud prevention.

Edith Cresson, France
Responsibilites: Science, research and development. Joint Research Centre. Human resources, education, training and youth.

Ritt Bjerregaard, Denmark
Responsibilites: Environment: nuclear safety.

Monika Wulf-Mathies, Germany
Responsibilites: Regional policies. Relations with the Committee of the Regions. Cohesion Fund (in agreement with Neil Kinnock and Ritt Bjerregaard).

Neil Kinnock, Britain
Responsibilites: Transport (including trans-European networks).

Mario Monti, Italy
Responsibilites: Internal market. Financial services and financial integration. Customs. Taxation.

Franz Fischler, Austria
Responsibilites: Agriculture and rural development.

Emma Bonino, Italy
Responsibilites: Fisheries. Consumer policy. European Community Humanitarian Office (ECHO).

Yves Thibault de Silguy, France
Responsibilites: Economic and financial affairs. Monetary matters (with the President).

Erkki Liikanen, Finland
Responsibilites: Budget. Personnel and administration. Translation and in-house computer services.

Christos Papoutsis, Greece
Responsibilites: Energy and Euratom Supply Agency. Small business: tourism.

Committees of the European Parliament

There are currently committees on:

1. Foreign Affairs and Security
   sub-committee on security and disarmament
   sub-committee on human rights
2. Agriculture and Rural Development
3. Budgets
4. Economic and Monetary Affairs and Industrial Policy
   sub-committee on monetary affairs
5. Energy, Research and Technology
6. External Economic Relations
7. Legal Affairs and Citizens' Rights
8. Social Affairs, Employment and the Working Environment
9. Regional Policy, Regional Planning and Relations with Regional and Local Authorities
10. Transport and Tourism
11. The Environment, Public Health and Consumer Protection
12. Culture, Youth, Education and the Media
13. Development and Co-operation
14. Civil Liberties
15. Budgetary Control
16. Institutional Affairs
17. Fisheries
18. Rules of Procedure, the Verification of Credentials and Immunities
19. Women's Rights
20. Petitions

Information Sources

European Commission Offices

England
Jean Monnet House
8 Storey's Gate
London SW1P 3AT
Tel: 0171-973 1992

Wales
4 Cathedral Street
Cardiff CF1 9SG
Tel: 01222-371 631

Scotland
9 Alva Street
Edinburgh EH2 4PH
Tel: 0131-225 2058

Northern Ireland
Windsor House
9–15 Bedford Street
Belfast BT2 7EG
Tel: 01232-240 708

Ireland
39 Molesworth Street
Dublin 2
Tel: (00 353) 1 712 244

US information centres
2100 M Street NW
Suite 707
Washington DC 20037
Tel: (001 USA) (202) 862-9500

305 East 47th Street
3 Dag Hammerskjöld Plaza
New York, NY 10017
Tel: (001 USA) (212) 371-3804

For information in other Member States, there is EU representation in all the capital cities, as well as Berlin and Munich for Germany, Marseilles in France, Barcelona in Spain, and Milan in Italy. There are also offices in Japan, Switzerland, Venezuela and Chile. Information is also available on the Internet under the heading 'Europa', though as yet not all topics are fully covered. Legislation that is being currently considered is published on the Internet, together with a diary of the major institutions' activities in the near future.

European Information Centres

These centres offer up-to-date information on the EU, with special reference to small and medium-sized enterprises, on subjects such as public contracts, company law and EU funding.

Belfast
European Business Information
    Centre
LEDU House
Upper Galwally
Belfast BT8 4TB
Tel: 01232-491 031

Birmingham
European Business Centre
Chamber of Commerce House
75 Harborne Road
Birmingham B15 3DH
Tel: 0121-455 0268

Bradford
WYEBIC
Economic Development Unit
2nd Floor, Mercury House
4 Manchester Road
Bradford BD5 0QL
Tel: 01274-754 262

Brighton/Hove
Sussex Chamber of Commerce
169 Church Road
Hove BN3 2AS
Tel: 01273-326 282

Bristol
Bristol Chamber of Commerce
16 Clifton Park
Bristol BS8 3BY
Tel: 0117-973 7373

Cardiff
Wales Euro Info Centre
UWCC Guest Building
PO Box 430
Cardiff CF1 3XT
Tel: 01222-229 525

Exeter
EIC South West
Reed Hall
University of Exeter
Exeter EX4 4QR
Tel: 01392-214 085

Glasgow
Euro Info Centre Ltd
21 Bothwell Street
Glasgow G2 7HY
Tel: 0141-221 0999

Hull
Humberside European Business
    Information Centre
Brynmor Jones Library
University of Hull
Cottingham Road
Hull HU6 7RX
Tel: 01482-465 935

Inverness
European Business Services
20 Bridge Street
Inverness IV1 1QR
Tel: 01463-702 560

Leeds
Mid-Yorkshire EIC
Leeds Metropolitan University
    Library
Calverley Street
Leeds LS1 3HE
Tel: 0113-283 3126

Leicester
EIC
10 York Road
Leicester LE1 5TS
Tel: 0116-255 9944

Liverpool
EIC North-West
Liverpool Central Libraries
William Brown Street
Liverpool L3 8EW
Tel: 0151-298 1928

London
London Chamber of Commerce
33 Queen Street
London EC4R 1AP
Tel: 0171-489 1992

Maidstone
Kent EIC
Springfield
Maidstone ME14 2LL
Tel: 01622-694 109

Manchester
Manchester Business Link
Churchgate House
56 Oxford Street
Manchester M60 7BL
Tel: 0161-237 4000

Newcastle
c/o Northern Development
    Company
Great North House
Sandyford Road
Newcastle-upon-Tyne
    NE1 8ND
Tel: 0191-261 0026

Norwich
Norfolk Chamber of Commerce
112 Barrack Street
Norwich NR3 1UB
Tel: 01603-625 977

Nottingham
EIC
309 Haydn Road
Nottingham NG5 1DG
Tel: 0115-962 4624

Sheffield
South Yorkshire EIC
The Library
Sheffield Hallam University
Pond Street
Sheffield S1 1WB
Tel: 0114-253 2126

Slough
Thames Valley EIC
Commerce House
2–6 Bath Road
Slough SL1 3SB
Tel: 01753-577 877

Southampton
Southern Area EIC
Civic Centre
Southampton SO9 4XP
Tel: 01703-832 866

Stafford
Staffordshire European
    Business Centre
Shire Hall
Market Street
Stafford ST16 2LQ
Tel: 01785-222 300

Telford
Shropshire and Staffordshire EIC
Business Link
Stafford Park 4
Telford TF3 3BA
Tel: 01952-208 213